Michael H

RENT BOYS

A HISTORY FROM ANCIENT TIMES TO THE PRESENT

© 2015

The inspiration of my books dates from the French Revolution with its Declaration of the Rights of Man in 1789, the end of homophobia in 1791, followed by the right of each man to marry the boy of his choice in 2013, the whole confirmed, in the States, by the American Supreme Court. My books include: *Cellini, Caravaggio, Cesare Borgia, Renaissance Murders, TROY, Argo, Greek Homosexuality, Roman Homosexuality, Renaissance Homosexuality, Alcibiades the Schoolboy, Henry III, Louis XIII, Buckingham, The Essence of Being Gay* and *Gay Genius*. I live in the South of France.

DEDICATION

This book is dedicated to Alex Stevens and Johan Volny. Wonders.

INTRODUCTION

This book spans the history of rent boys from the Greeks, the most famous of which was Alcibiades, through Rome to the Renaissance where a rent boy was made a cardinal and where others were responsible for the most appalling murders of the period. Victorian England was a hustler's heaven, and Berlin and Paris their Mecca. The book is about boys who sold themselves and about the men who bought them--often the same: selling their services when young, consumers when old. The book ends with the actors of yesteryear and the escort services of today.

''Let it be known that homosexuals are not cowards,'' Willem Arondeus cried out before a Nazi firing squad in 1943. The purpose of my books, all my books, from *Homosexual Heroes* to *Rent Boys*, is the affirmation that homosexuals, from da Vinci to Nietzsche, have done their part in the enlightenment and advancement of civilization. We are no more, but certainly no less, than those who have made this world a passionate, colorful, *unique* adventure.

This is adult reading: *Caveat emptor,* Let the buyer beware.

CONTENTS

GREEK TIMES

RENT-BOY SEX IN GREECE
Page 5

AESCHINES AGAINST TIMARCHUS
346 B.C.
Page 6

ROMAN TIMES

SEX IN GREECE AND ROME
Page 8

RENT-BOY SEX IN ROME
Page 23

SATYRICON
Page 26

RENAISSANCE TIMES

SCIPIONE BORGHESE
Page 28

JULIUS III
Page 29

CENCI MURDER
Page 31

CARLO GESUALDO
Page 33

ROMANTIC TIMES

THOMAS BECKFORD
Page 35

BYRON
Page 50

VICTORIAN TIMES

VICTORIAN RENT BOYS
Page 68

WHITE SWAN SCANDAL
Page 69

CLEVELAND STREET TELEGRAM SCANDAL
Page 71

THE SINS OF THE CITIES OF THE PLAIN
Page 73

ROGER CASEMENT
Page 74

MODERN TIMES

JACQUES D'ADELSWÄRD-FERSEN
Page 86

AMERICA 1920s
BERLIN 1930s
Page 93

ESCORT SERVICES
Page 102

ACTORS AND AGENTS
Page 104

POSTSCRIPT
Page 122

SOURCES
Page 122

GREEK TIMES

RENT-BOY SEX IN GREECE

The golden rule in Greece was that the man was active and the boy passive, and when the boy became a man the roles were reversed. Rent boys could lengthen their time of availability by a meticulous shaving or depilation of chin and ass cheeks, and pomades, friends helping each other out in the maneuvers.

Male brothels were set up for those who were no longer young, whose role had been to educate a boy in the ways of war and citizenship, expulsing their lust as freely and often as they wished, with each insemination accompanied by some new aspect of learning, so that the boy would successfully become a man himself, and a model Athenians, all of which demanded time, courtship and gifts, and was a highly serious investment. Those boys who left this natural path and received money and/or gifts in return, forfeited their rights as a citizen in that they could no longer publicly participate in a governing organization, the Boule of 400 set up to council the Assembly, the courts, the Aeropagus, etc.

Men's needs were recognized even by Athens' foremost leaders, and Solon himself established brothels outside of which boys stood nude in order for the client to see exactly what he was buying for his obol (an obol, 1/6th of a drachma in the 5th century, to 1 ½ drachma in the 4th--estimated amounts authorized by the state for sex)--or whatever the price, as it was at times fixed, but varied through the centuries. Male prostitution was a trade nearly like another, and Theophrastus in his *Characters* lists the occupation of pimp alongside other trades: cook, innkeeper, et al.

As today, cruising areas in Athens were the port, the Piraeus; the market and the Kerameikos (the site of a huge cemetery); Lycabettus (a pine-covered hill), as well as outside gymnasiums, barracks and wooded areas similar to our parks. At times it was a free exchange of those out to mutually help in expulsing their lust, at time it cost money, at times it began as the first and ended up as the second, as the boy asked for a small financial gift, especially from older men. Foreigners and metics made their living by selling their asses, some Greek boys too, with the resultant restrictions of their civil rights (for Athenians).

Free sex demanded some degree of physical attraction and entailed mutual masturbation, intercrural and/or anal stimulation (one often led to the other); paid sex had the advantage of quick service with no time lost, supplemented by fellatio, rare otherwise because considered degrading, a highly pleasurable adjunct, effortless for the receiver.

In a sense this was democracy in action, as it was "democratic" for each man to have access to pleasure, and Solon was said to have used the taxes gathered in the construction of a temple to Aphrodite herself, the goddess of love, although a temple to Apollo would have been more appropriate, at least for taxes from male prostitutes πόρνοι. Prostitution was nonetheless considered socially degrading for an Athenian boy, the reason for his loss of certain civic rights. The act of his selling himself for the pleasure of others was a loss of dignity, and if he sold himself, would he not as easily sell-out Athens? In less polite terms, Athenians knew that boys who offered their asses to all comers were no more than "dissolute buzzards," as Polybius wrote (see Sources).

It is possible that the price varied according to what men demanded of the boys, and according to the beauty and youth of the lads. A huge difference between male and female prostitution was that boys were used during their adolescents, while women could last far longer, and in fact the older the woman the more she was experienced, which led women to believe that men really preferred them, because once a boy was no longer as soft and hairless as a woman he was rejected.

Lucian (see Sources) wrote in his *Affairs of the Heart* that men who sought sex with boys over twenty wanted mutual love, for by then "their limbs were hard and manly, their once soft chins had become rough and covered with bristles, and their thighs were sullied with hair."

Socrates set free the sexual slave Phaedo of Elis who gave his name to Socrates' *Phaedo*. It is not known if Socrates used the boy sexually.

A boy soliciting sex.

AESCHINES AGAINST TIMARCHUS

346 B.C.

An Athenian could do as he wished with a slave, a foreigner and a metic sexually, he could have sex with another Athenian, but he could not sell himself unless willing to give up all civil rights. If he became a rent boy he could no longer appear before any assembly and plead or ask for aid for any cause. If he ever hid his having sold himself and then appeared before an assembly and was caught at it, he would be stoned.

Aeschines' father was a schoolteacher and Aeschines, born in Athens, tried teaching before distinguishing himself in the army, and finally becoming a government official. As such he went to conclude a treaty between Athens and Philip of Macedon. He was accused of selling himself to Philip by a certain Timarchus, an accusation of treason that Timarchus brought before the Assembly, the penalty for which was death. Aeschines struck back by bringing a counter-suit against Timarchus claiming that he had no right to speak before the Assembly as he had sold himself on the waterfront of the Piraeus when a boy. Timarchus was thusly forced to stand trial, giving us the first and only full account of male sexual relations in ancient Athens.

Aeschines began his speech by stating that Timarchus knew he had no right to appeal to the Assembly because ''he knows that we live in a democracy, which means we live under the rule of law. Thanks to these laws a teacher cannot open a schoolroom or the gymnastic trainer the wrestling school before sunrise, and the law commands them to close the doors before sunset, for the law is suspicious of men being alone with a boy, or in the dark with him. No person who is older than the boys shall be permitted to enter a changing room while they are there. If anyone enters in violation of this prohibition, he shall be punished with death. The superintendents of the gymnasia shall under no conditions allow anyone who has reached the age of manhood to be alone with the boys. A teacher who permits this and fails to keep such a person out of the gymnasium will be liable to the penalties prescribed for the seduction of freeborn youths--death.

''If any boy is let out for hire as a prostitute, whether it be by father or brother or uncle or guardian, or by anyone else who has control of him, prosecution is not to be against the boy himself, but against the man who let him out for hire and the man who hired him. Moreover, the law frees a son, when he has become a man, from all obligation to support or to furnish a home to a father by whom he has been hired out for prostitution.

''As soon as the young man has been registered in the list of citizens, and knows the laws of the state, and is able to distinguish between right and wrong, he is responsible for his acts. If he then prostitutes himself, which is a reckless sin against his own body, and then seeks to address the Assembly or Senate, he shall be put to death.

''Now, a certain Misgolas got Timarchus into his own home and because Timarchus was well developed, young, lewd and in the very bloom of youth, Misgolas did what he wanted to do and Timarchus wanted to have done.'' Aeschines gives no detailed information as to what the sexual acts consisted of so as not to shame himself or the Assembly. Yet he gave a list of men who were shining, pious examples of how men should behave. Three of these men were Themistocles and Aristides who were fighting for the same boy, the outcome of which was Aristides' expulsion from Athens, while Solon wrote this:

> Blessed is the man sweaty from the gym,
> Having muscles, supple, strong and slim,
> Goes home where he may drink wine and play,
> With a fair boy on his chest all day.

Meaning that Aeschines was in no way speaking against male-male sexual couplings, but was referring exclusively to the law against a rent boy later serving and addressing free Athenian citizens. He then goes on about Homer: ''I will speak first of Homer, whom we rank among the oldest and wisest of the poets. Although he speaks in many places of Patroclus and Achilles, he hides their love and avoids giving a name to their friendship, thinking that the exceeding greatness of their affection is manifest to his hearers who are educated men. His lament following the death of Patrocles is proof of his love for him.''

Aeschines goes on about beautiful boys who hadn't stooped to prostitution, going so far as to give a list of their names. The trial ends thusly:

''But your bestiality, Timarchus, is known to one and all. For just as we recognize the athlete, even without visiting the gymnasia, by looking at his bodily vigor, even so we recognize the prostitute, even without being present at his act, by his shamelessness, his effrontery, and his habits.''

Aeschines finishes by reminding the Assembly that when they return home their young sons will ask them how the case was decided. ''Does the Assembly want to tell them that it is now permitted for a boy to defile his body with the sins of a woman (being used as a woman)? Punish this one man. Do not wait until you have a multitude to punish.''

Timarchus was indeed found guilty. He left his trial and hanged himself.

ROMAN TIMES

SEX IN GREECE AND ROME

All historical sources conclude that the Romans couldn't care less if a man stuck his dick in a girl or a boy: it just didn't matter. Caesar himself was known to be a man to every woman, a woman to every man. His soldiers sang ditties to that effect as they marched along, perhaps not always to Caesar's amusement; in fact, Caesar was far more sensitive about losing his hair than having lost his cherry, when young, to King Nicomedes who happened to have been a Bithynian like Antinous, and like Antinous Nicomedes was noted for the dimensions of his member. The words hetero and homo didn't exist yet because the distinction between them was immaterial.

Priapus and His Weight in Gold mural scene

Whereas Greek boys were encouraged to have older lovers and to learn from them, the Romans had sex for pleasure as long as the participants respected two iron-clad principles (although, as we all well know, all iron-clad principles are made to be disregarded): A Roman male could not have sex with another Roman male. If he was horny and a slave (or a foreigner or anyone else, as long as he wasn't a Roman) passed by, he was fair game. The second principle was that a Roman male had to do the penetrating. It was he who was *vir*ile (*vir* meaning man in Latin). A corollary to the two principles was the very strong preference for young smooth hairless bodies, often between the ages of 14 and 20, marked by the onset of down on the boy's cheeks (permissible too on his butt cheeks). Greek boys had Greek lovers, often many, from whom the boys gained the key to life: *knowledge*. The boys were normally passive, the men active, and when the boys became men, the roles were reversed: they took on a boy of their own, their belovèd, and they became the boy's lover and teacher. There was also a practical side to Greek love. A lover would never ever show weakness before his belovèd and vice versa, which made them the fiercest fighting force the world has ever known.

The Romans and Greeks practiced vaginal and anal penetration, intercrural insertion, fellatio and cunnilingus, the last two rare. Mutual masturbation and circle jerks were rarely mentioned because they were so common between schoolboys, a little like boys pissing together, and perhaps also because this took place between Roman boys. Parents despaired of keeping their sons, if they were beautiful, chaste. Roman boys did have access to slaves, just like their elders did, on whom they could practice intercourse, intercrural or anal. As today, the Romans associated male/male relations with Greece (in France one says, for the English Go Fuck Yourself: *Va te faire voir chez les Grecs).* In the same way that one drinks anything when thirsty or eats the food offered when hungry, one will go with any male slave or foreigner when he has a hard-on. Diogenes the Cynic says that of the three appetites, food, drink and sex, sex is the easiest to fulfill as one need only rub oneself to obtain instant satisfaction.

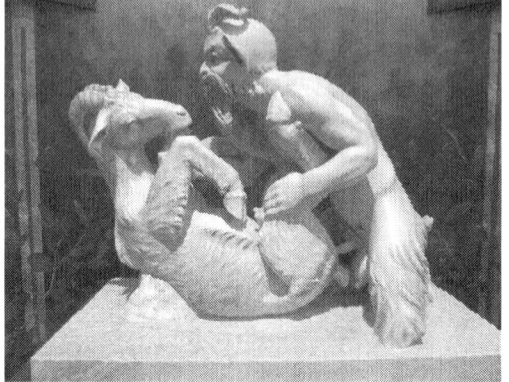

Pan copulating with a goat.

Sex was found in brothels and latrines and taverns, parks and gardens and any other place sheltered from public view. Hadrian's successor, Lucius Verus, opened a tavern in his own home in order to create a climate for debauch. Male prostitutes showed their wares in parks and gardens as they do today, and many turned to acting to supplement their incomes, as did Hadrian's favorite Pylades.

Lucius Verus

    As just being a wife was enough status for most women, men were free to look elsewhere for pleasure. In Rome love was always in the air (just like today). The Romans had adopted many of the Greek gods and their myths, especially those which dealt with Apollo and Hyacinth, Hercules and Hylas, Achilles and Patroclus, Zeus and his cupbearer and bedmate Ganymede. Antinous' role was strikingly similar to that played by Ganymede, and as he was Greek he was a safe foreigner, although it's doubtful that Hadrian would have turned him away should he have been a Roman citizen. The Greeks were not obliged to look for sex in gardens or taverns or back alleys. They had gymnasiums where they could openly entice boys, although not those under age 18. Rich parents sent slaves to accompany their sons to and from the gym. Sex between boys was so current that we have the story of the Greek boy who didn't share his schoolmates' interest in men. He prayed to Zeus so that he too could be moved by the love of boys, but when this failed to happen, he committed suicide.

Two men, one woman--mural

A huge difference between the Greeks and the Romans (if historians, after two thousand years, are correct; let us not forget that there isn't one word in Homer concerning homosexual relationships) was that the Greeks preferred their boys with modest members, the perfect size to fit the anus, whereas the Romans followed the cult of Priapus, and, as today, thought that bigger was always better. Clapping could be heard in the Roman baths when a man of healthy dimensions paraded through the corridors. One Roman, Cotta, was known to invite only guests to his lavish dinners whom he had first seen at the baths--a word often on his lips was donkey. Presumably, even heteros today show deferential admiration for those who show more manliness than they do themselves, which does not necessarily have anything to do with the desire to be penetrated. Roman boys often wore phallic amulets to protect them from the evil eye, and even today Roman men and boys quickly touch their balls to ward off evil, as when, for example, they see a passing priest.

Some hoopla developed concerning the roles of the Greek lover and his belovèd. Lovers didn't just fall in love with any boy, but only those who showed intelligence and maturity. The sexual link was ephemeral and came to an end with the growing of a first beard. From then on the boy and lover became loyal friends and remained so throughout their lives. Love was to be simple and undebauched, built on education and physical maintenance. But if this were true, wondered Cicero, why did lovers only fall in love with handsome youths and never ugly ones?

Boys, then as now, were mantraps: The poet Tibullus tells us that we have no chance against tender youths, who give us ample reason to love them. This boy is pleasing due to the masterly control he has over his horse; this other one causes our hearts to flutter when he breaks the surface of the water, showing his snow-white chest and nipples; so and so captures us by his daring; such and such by his peaches-and-cream complexion. At times youths objected for the form when men made advances, even menacing to tell their fathers if the men didn't cease. But once bridled, and the man could find rest after expulsing his lust, it was the boy who sought more, awaking the man from sleep by the gentle entreating of his buttocks. Again satisfied, man and boy plunged back into the arms of Morpheus for an hour before the boy asked if the man would like to do it again. The man would, but when the boy stirred still again, an hour later, it was the man who threatened the boy, ''If you don't stop I'll tell your daddy!''

Pan and Nymph

    Boys also lacked fidelity. The poet presents a letter sent from one Kurnos, a Greek, to his lover Timaleus, away at war. ''Dear Timaleus, it is I, Kurnos. Many a friend has come and gone since you left, but it is to you that my thoughts return. Whenever I see Themis' horses, I think of my friend Timaleus. Remember how we stole rides before Eos' early light, and galloped across the fields like a single rider on his dapple mare--I've quite forgotten her name. She's grown too old to support one as sturdy as I, but she foaled just after you went away, and the little colt has long since borne my weight. Do you regret my sending you on campaign? I only stayed a month with Saurus and from then after missed only you. Come back home, my dear friend, and do not upbraid me harshly, for it is as the poet said: 'Boys and horses are the same. A horse does not cry for his rider thrown into the dust, but carries another man and eats his corn; a boy, too, only loves his current friend.' ''

    The role of a boy wasn't always easy either. Men liked them soft enough to caress, but not so soft as to be effeminate. Boys might relish being penetrated, but not enough to be mistaken for a woman. If the boy seemed too eager he could open himself to abuse, as men abused girls who were too available. Boys were often believed to be easily impaled because the anal muscles were supple, due to the fact that they hadn't as yet turned into real men. But rent boys were often called upon to sodomize men who lusted for anal contact, as they had when young, because their anuses itched for what only a penis could scratch.

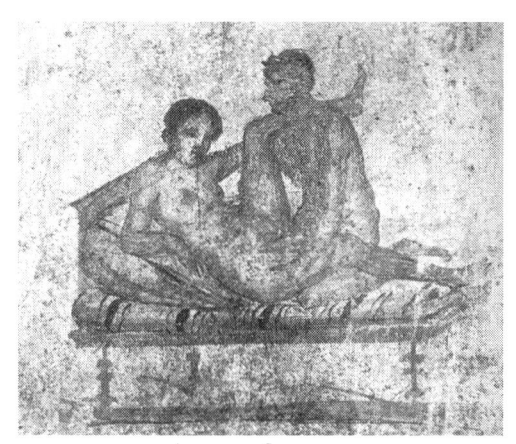

A mural scene

Fellatio and cunnilingus were both looked down upon as being unclean (as if sodomy were any better). The former, fellatio, was often associated with grown men with beards. Women were there for fucking, boys for sodomy and bearded men for cock sucking. Another degrading aspect was the use of sex to further one's advancement. From multiple sources we learn that this was Hadrian's way with Trajan's entourage: he advanced through fucking the emperor's influential friends, and by being fucked by them. But given the known promiscuous nature of Trajan's court, and the incredible sexual arousal in a climate of lustful males, most of whom were not simply Trajan's buddies but youths recruited to fulfill the needs of the emperor and his associates, Hadrian's task had certainly not been arduous--unless it went on and on until physical exhaustion and/or discomfort.

Socrates warns about kissing Alcibiades' handsome son: ''The beast they call young and handsome is more dangerous than a scorpion. You needn't touch a boy as you do a scorpion to be poisoned. A boy, with just a look, can make you mad from a distance. So when you see a beautiful boy run for your life, take a year's holiday elsewhere as it will take that long to heal you.''

The Greek ideal of how fathers should raise their sons was, as usual, based on the gods. Zeus, for example, had excellent relations with his sons Hermes and Apollo. Here the poet reveals a scene in which Zeus is explaining to Apollo just how smart Hermes is: '' 'I've never seen anyone so clever. A while back, for instance, Hermes and I were scrounging around Earth on some business or other--no, not what you're thinking; there were no petticoats involved--and being hungry and tired we stopped in at a peasant's hut along the way. Well, Son, you know how lowly and miserably those humans live. I had to destroy them once by sending that great flood, so sick had I become of seeing their despicable ways. I can't figure it out. They have everything to make them happy: physically they are as perfectly formed and as sound as are we; they have the same brain and heart; it should be as easy for them to love and be loved as it is for us. But what do we see on Earth? Tortured faces, worried expressions, selfish acts. I could forgive them their weaknesses were they to at least take part in life. But no. They scurry around like sheep, their heads down for fear the heavens may fall. And when Death beckons, they trudge off to the cold blackness of the tomb, they who could have known light, warmth and laughter during their ephemeral existence

' ''Anyway,'' continued Zeus, ''Hermes and I stopped at some peasant's hovel and to our astonishment we were hospitably offered warm wine and vittles. To thank the old man, Hermes and I asked him to confide his heart's innermost wish. The poor old fellow sighed and said that although he was impotent and his wife long dead, his heart's desire was to have a son.

' ''Now, I would have instructed him to eat a certain potent mushroom that has wondrous regenerative powers and then get himself a mistress. But not Hermes. After some thought he told the old man to go to his wife's grave and take out her bones. He was then to sacrifice a bull to Almighty Myself, skin the hide into which he would place his wife's bones, piss on the remains, and bury the hide and its contents in his wife's grave. At the end of nine months he was to return and dig it all up.

' ''The old man did as instructed, and when he returned nine months later he found a boy at the bottom of the pit, swaddled in the old hide. We named him 'Orion', which is Greek for 'He-Who-Makes-Water' and, by extension, urine.' '' (2)

In the ancient world, as today, boys and men knew pining, tears, longing, despair, self-sacrifice--the entire panoply of sentiments. In Thebes the Sacred Band was formed, 300 lovers and their belovèds, fed at public expense and housed on the acropolis, they formed a group of warriors who would sacrifice themselves at the snap of a finger for their companions. Love between men was so special in Thebes that it was, says Plato, illegal for anyone to maintain that sex between men was *not* beautiful. Thanks to the Sacred Band Thebes freed itself from Spartan domination, until it was totally destroyed by Alexander the Great, he who was said to have known defeat only once in his life, when confronting the thighs of his lover Hephaestion.

Naturally, had there been only homosexuals in Thebes, Thebans would have died out. Plutarch relates the story of a rich Theban woman who arranged the kidnapping of a handsome ephebe that she then kept at her side until he understood that she was as interested in his welfare as she was her sexual satisfaction. She married the lad, to the fury of his male suitors. There is the story of Heracles' passage through Thebes where he slept, during a single night, with the forty-nine virgin daughters of the same father. The fiftieth daughter refused him and in anger he sentenced her to remain a virgin until the end of her life. Girls, however, got the best of Heracles when his boyfriend, the beautiful Hylas, abandoned him for nymphs that resided in a spring (which may have meant, in reality, that at some time during their relationship Hylas drowned).

At any rate, a good father always had a ready tale for his son's ears. Zeus told Hermes about the Trojan War, but as the story was long and the boy appeared to be asleep ... well ... let the poet finish: ''Almighty Zeus interrupted his story and looked down at this son. Hermes' arm and head rested unmoving on Zeus' leg. Zeus thought he had fallen asleep, and softly tried to disengage himself. But Hermes raised his head. There was the same look of intelligence and anticipation, although with anxiety least Almighty Father wish not to continue. Zeus hadn't the heart to abridge his promise to tell the story of the Great War. So after taking a few moments out while he put more tree trunks on the fire, stopped the moon and stars in their course and issued orders to Sleep--who owed him a favor--to make this night thrice, he returned to his throne, Hermes again at this knees, and while running his fingers through his son's auburn locks, Almighty Father picked up the thread of his tale without the loss of a single strand.'' (2)

Augustus continually tongue-whipped the nobility because they weren't showing the example to the people by producing more progeny, which meant more farmers, more government servants and, especially, more soldiers. It must never be forgotten that for Rome incessant war was a source of wealth in various goods, land (especially land for soldiers upon their retirement), agricultural products and slaves--slaves that ran the economy thanks to their work, but also because they were often the teachers and philosophers who gave direction to Roman life and culture, and were receptacles for Roman lust.

Hadrian was absorbed by mysticism, the occult, fortune telling and the like which could not only caste the spells that could bring one a lover or assure the death of an enemy, but could also help in one's sexual performance--supernatural aphrodisiacs. Pornography was an aid and walls were often covered with erotic frescos. Prostitution was legal, public and practiced everywhere. Males were naturally attracted to boys as well as girls, and it must not be forgotten that words for homosexual or heterosexual didn't exist in any form, although there were words for effeminacy. Again: virility comes from the Latin *vir* meaning manly, but is also found in the word virtue, meaning that it was appropriate to control one's sexual appetites. (This is what the Romans wrote, but I have my doubts concerning the ''virtue'' angle.)

Pederasty referred to, in ancient Greece, young men, not young boys. There was, naturally, no *legal* age in Greece. The boys involved were military age, which infers that they had left boyhood. In Greece pederasty was simply the socially accepted erotic friendship between a man and a boy, a boy being between the ages of 15 to 17 (many Greek poets refer to 16 as the perfect age for the belovèd). In Crete it seems to have been a vital ingredient in military life, sanctioned by Zeus himself, an active pederast. Many scholars have found it strange that it was not commented on at all in Homer (a reason, perhaps, why Hadrian eventually turned away from Homer to the benefit of other writers such as Herodotus, Plato, Athenaeus and Xenophon--Xenophon whom Hadrian adored). In all other aspects of Greek life pederasty was clearly apparent: nude athletics, nude sculptures of ephebes (kouroi), historically famous cohorts of men and boys such as the Sacred Band of Thebes, as well as--with very few exceptions--the utter exclusion of women.

From this distance in time it's hard to pin down the behavior of the belovèd. Some poets claim that his role was passive in the sense that he contented himself with being beautiful, looking meekly at the ground as his lover greats him, allowing the man to stroke his cheek and gently nudge his genitals through the boy's chiton, the light tunic he wore that fell to the knees. Today this would seem erotic and daring, but also how arousing! Perhaps the lad did feel he had to play a submissive role, but I'm sure all masks fell away while he was being, later and in private, tenderly caressed by his lover.

In Crete a boy seems to have been abducted by a lover who, in concord with the boy's friends, takes the lad into the countryside where they spend two idyllic months hunting, feasting and exhausting their young bodies. The belovèd is then returned home with the symbolic gifts of military dress, an ox and a drinking cup (and whatever else the man might wish him to have, gifts the expense of which would depend on the man's resources). Interestingly, the boy was then known by a Greek word meaning "he who stands ready," perhaps signifying Ganymede who, after being abducted by Zeus, stood ready, at the god's side, to serve him food and drink. It's interesting too to note that the boy's father was keep informed of each stage of his son's abduction and, indeed, his great wish was to have a son who would be handsome enough to attract a suitable suitor--one influential enough to give the boy a boost into the better classes, knowing full well that his boy would be the object of sexual passion, as the father had himself been as a boy.

Boys in Greece were free to choose their suitors, while the boys' sisters had to comply with theirs father's wishes, wishes based on political and economic advantages. The boys received continual gifts and tender attention from their lovers, the girls were paid for and sent to the kitchen or the bed according to their husband's needs. Girls remained virgin until marriage and remained loyal to their husbands. Boys could have as many relationships with other boys and men as they wished, each serving as a step upwards in the boys' advancement through society. As related, the same was true for Hadrian who sought influence with Trajan by plowing the buttocks of the emperor's consorts or allowing access to his own. In Athens as well as in Rome boys and their multiple lovers remained friends, often throughout their entire lives.

Prostitutes served as an alternate form of sexual outlet. Romans and Greeks had the choice of women, girls, wives, men, boys and pleasuring themselves. The only difference, as said, was that Roman men could not have sex with other Roman men or women (other than one's own wife or husband), but only with foreigners, slaves and rent boys--a rule certainly broken on occasion. And they had to be the top, in today's parlance, never the bottom. In Greece anything went down as normal and good, although throughout all time the penetrator has always been more respected than the penetrated. Prostitutes were looked down upon and Roman or Greek nobles thought to have sold their wares were tainted through the rest of their lives. Caesar himself never lived down the accusation, certainly true, that he was King Nicomedes' boy while ambassador to Bithynia. In Athens the politician Aeschines lost power when accused of having been a rent boy in his youth.

Virtus, manliness, was the quality that drove the Roman state and gave the Romans *imperium*, power, over their women, over foreigners and foreign countries, and over their slaves. This manliness was tied to sexual dominance. A Roman man was expected to penetrate the rest of the world as he did a mistress and his boys, and it was he who would decide who would be allowed to penetrate the females in his household.

As in relationships today, then, too, one could turn on one's lover. There is the example of Philip of Macedon, Alexander the Great's father. When Philip was a boy he was sent to Thebes and placed under the care of Pammenes, a great general and boy-lover who immediately reserved the young and willing prince for his bed. Pammenes is known for criticizing Nestor's role in the Trojan War because Nestor organized the men according to their country and not in groups of lovers and their belovèds, groups that would have fought to the death before letting down their loved-ones. No act was more valued than giving one's life for one's belovèd.

Later, when Philip was king of Macedon, his general Pausanias came to him with the complaint that he had been forcefully sodomized. Pausanias felt that he had the king's ear because they had been lovers when young. Pausanias claimed that he had had relations with a boy who killed himself when Pausanias threw him over for another. The boy's former lover, a certain Attalus, decided to wreck vengeance on Pausanias by inviting him to a banquet, during which he forcefully raped Pausanian after getting him drunk. Pausanias hoped that King Philip would avenge the outrage by killing Attalus, but Attalus was both an essential general in Philip's army and the father of Philip's wife. So to placate Pausanias, Philip named him to his personal guard, affording Pausanias the proximity he needed to drive a dagger into Philip's chest--thus opening the way for Philip's son, the Great Alexander. Pausanias, in turn, was cut down by the rest of Philip's guard.

In Plato's *Symposium* we learn that man-and-boy love was advantageous because no army could overcome the bond between lovers, and it worked in the favor of democracy because no despotic ruler was more powerful than the loyalty between men and their boys. We have the case of Harmodius and Aristogeiton: Hippias and Hipparchus were joint dictators in Athens. Hipparchus fancied Harmodius who refused his advances. To gain revenge, Hipparchus refused to let Harmodius' sister take part in the Panathenaea Games, accusing her of not being a virgin, a requirement for the games. Harmodius and his lover Aristogeiton decided to rid Athens of the dictatorship and thusly redeem the honor of Harmodius' sister. With daggers hidden in their chitons, the boys fell on Hipparchus at the foot of the Acropolis, stabbing him to death. Hipparchus' guards immediately killed Harmodius and Aristogeiton was captured. While being tortured to reveal any coconspirators, Aristogeiton promised to tell the truth if Hippias would promise him clemency, sealed with a handshake. When Hippias complied, Aristogeiton laughed at his having shaken the hand of his own brother's murderer. Hippias, mad with fury, thrust his dagger into Aristogeiton's throat (1).

Plato claimed that the ideal nation would be based on lovers, because no lover would ever dishonor his belovèd. To the contrary, he would do everything in his power to build him up, to educate him, to do for him all that was virtuous and good and honorable. All the great gods, all of them with the one exception of Ares, god of war, were lovers to their belovèds. (Ares was too unfeeling to appreciate tender friendships: he killed and maimed, maddening men so they would take nursing babies from their mothers and dash their brains against walls or tree trunks.) The poet Theognis justified his own love of boys by relating, to friends, the story of how Zeus had abducted Ganymede. As in Rome, the Greeks too were unaware of the concept of sexual orientation. Men quite simply did what they wanted to do (as the enlightened ones do to this day--as long as laws are respected, naturally). Only the role in the act was of importance. In Rome and in Athens the penetrator was masculine, adult and of high social status; the penetrated was a youth or, if not, he was categorized as being effeminate or socially inferior. Not only did men share a sexual relationship with boys, they saw to it that boys were educated in the Greek way, meaning in the responsibilities that would be theirs in manhood. The period between the moment the man took a liking to a boy and the moment he quenched his desire, could be several weeks or months, giving the youth time to assure himself that the man had a genuine attachment for him, one that surpassed sexual lust. Normally the youth had pubic hair, but cases of boys being appropriated at age 12 were not unknown.

Such was Patroclus' role with his belovèd Achilles: friend, teacher and protector. The poet enters their sleeping chamber: ''Both arranged their clothes. Achilles slipped into the bed the first, and then Patroclus. Patroclus found his place against Achilles' side, his leg gently draped over his belovèd's thighs. Did Patroclus foresee his coming fate, a fate he knew he held in common with others, as he held in common the happiness that filled his heart at this moment, a happiness that was his, but one that others had known and would know again, and that long after he had become dust? He put his arm under his belovèd's head and leaned over him. Silently he searched the blue eyes, and finding his answer, he kissed the parted lips. Then he moved his head back and with one breath blew out the oil lamp, bringing down night, a celestial curtain.'' (2)

In Rome men may have preferred the passive role, desiring to be penetrated by their slaves, but such men were not considered as being *vir*, real-men: only the penetration of a handsome youth, by a man, was judged conventional. The use of perfume and cosmetics and others forms of effeminacy were tolerated by some men when they concerned youths, but not adult men. Roman boys and men were allowed male-slave-sexual-partners as a way of discharging one's lust, an alternative form to pleasuring oneself. The male-slave-sexual-partner was generally replaced, sooner or later, by a wife. The slave would then cut his hair short and join the domain of the other slaves. A slave boy could be castrated to preserve a youthful aspect, as Nero had castrated Sporus before marrying him. Naturally, slaves could service their mistresses as well as their masters. As with Caesar (and King Nicomedes), Roman males often went through stages during which they evolved from being sexually passive to sexually active. In one well-known case, involving a youth who did not manage the transition from passive to active, his father, Quintus Fabius Maximus Eburnus, had his son killed for being ''unchaste.'' The hypocrisy of the matter was that as a youth Fabius himself was called a ''chick'', signifying a boy-love-object. He had been known for his good looks and availability. His reaction towards his son was perhaps a counter-reaction against his own juvenile misdeeds. The satirist Juvenal states that rent boys were found in streets known to all, as well as the baths, especially valued as one could check out the potential of what one was buying. As previously mentioned, the key word for most same-sex-enthusiasts was ''hung''. Apuleius, the irreverent writer of *The Golden Ass*, mentions a banquet in the midst of which a ''*well-endowed*'' young man was fellated by all the participants.

Same-sex marriages were not legally recognized in Rome. The aforementioned Juvenal criticized them because he felt that one day they would be legalized. Nero purportedly married several men, Pythagoras and Sporus among them. Nero was the bride and wore a bridal veil, the men received a substantial dowry. Cicero accused Mark Antony of being a slut in his youth and the rent boy to one Curio. This is one of many reasons Antony insisted on Cicero's death the moment Antony gained power. The exquisite Emperor Elagabalus is reported to have married his charioteer, Hierocles, and the athlete Zoticus. He was assassinated at age 18.

Rapists were subject to death if they raped a woman, boy or man. Slaves, prostitutes and entertainers were public property, and as such couldn't be raped (even up to Shakespeare's time actors often rounded off their monthly earnings as rent boys). A man who was raped (anally or orally) was legally exempt from public stigma. It goes without saying that rape was the perfect vengeance, and according to some sources it occurred as often between men as it did between men and women among the Romans. When it happened to a Roman citizen it was thought to equal, in horror, parricide, the rape of a virgin or the robbing of a temple.

Augustus banned soldiers from marrying, a ban that held good for 200 years. Soldiers could not have sex among themselves in the same way that no Roman citizen could have sex with another Roman citizen outside of marriage. Many took mistresses and had children that they recognized after leaving the service. All turned to prostitutes of both sexes and gang rapes following military conquests. As with all other Roman citizens, a man was forbidden to lose his masculinity by allowing his body to be violated. The historian Polybius wrote that a soldier found guilty of being penetrated was clubbed to death. Polybius also tells us that men spent a *talent* for a male lover--$2,000. Plutarch recounts the story of the handsome recruit who was pursued by his commanding officer. He shunned the unwanted advances until the officer ordered him to, in effect, bend over. The recruit drew his sword and plunged it into the chest of the commander. Not only wasn't the recruit sentenced to death, the mandatory sentence, he was awarded the Crown for Bravery, the equivalent of today's Medal of Honor.

The poet Ausonius jokes about a threesome, stating that there were four acts of sin. ''How is that possible'' a friend asks, ''if there were only three?'' ''There is one man on either side, with the one in the middle doing double duty.''

It seems evident that due to the multiple ways of appeasing one's lust, Roman males put off marriage. Naturally, if a woman was of the high nobility and wealthy, she didn't remain without a husband for long, but with husbands seeking release with young girls and boys who were foreigners, slaves and/or prostitutes, and with one entering into adultery as freely and guiltlessly as did the Romans, the birth rate diminished to such an extent that the great Augustus never stopped chewing out the men who frequented his court. Finally, laws were drawn up, forcing men to marry at the very latest between the ages of 25 and 30, and to produce a child before age

26 if they wished to escape penalties. Women were to marry between ages 20 and 30, giving birth during her twentieth year. Men who fathered three children or more received rewards and rapid career advancement. As boys sought fortune by giving themselves to older men (an example being Marc Antony and the wealthy Curio whose relationship lasted so long that it was considered an unofficial marriage by some) in hopes of a rapid and rich inheritance, a law was passed allowing such legacies only from close relatives. Widows were obliged to marry within two years of their husbands' deaths and divorcees within 18 months. Also, Augustus, knowing that theaters were the preferred sites for men who hoped to waylay boys, set aside special sections where the boys could be accompanied by chaperons, an extremely difficult task as handsome boys always found a way to men who knew the art of flattery and knew of boys' ever present need for the sound of sweet jangling pocket change. Of course, Augustus too had been a beautiful boy and had certainly had his share of suitors. Where before one had looked the other way concerning adultery, now adulterers were punished with banishment or flogging. Augustus had his daughter Julia sent to rot on an island, as she was found to have spread her thighs for literally any virile male. Male/male relations were never punished, but the loss of one's seed between a boy's buttocks or through autoeroticism were considered a waste in times when the state needed kids, and plenty of them.

While Augustus lived an inspirational life of moderation in food, surroundings and sex, Rome--like Florence during the Renaissance--was more and more enticed by Hellenistic pederasty, although Roman sex often included men-on-men to a far greater degree than did the Greeks whose ideal was always boys and youths. Patrons like Maecenas and other wealthy boy-loving Hellenists, assured the survival of generations of poets, Martial, Catullus, Horace, Virgil et al., at least as long as they were young and available. We're told that Hadrian often drank and loved boys, but that he was never drunk and that he had never ever harmed a lad. The general, historian and poet Arrian, sent to Cappadocia by Hadrian, wrote the life of Alexander and gave advice in the Stoic tradition, advised against taking up with ballet boys but counseled that one should take one's pleasure decently with both sexes. Graffiti found from that time describes a cobbler and a rope maker who lived together and were buried together.

Lucius Apuleius is known for his book the *Golden Ass* in which a sorcerer accidently turns himself into an ass and has all kinds of Boccaccio-like adventures; but he's also noted for his youthful love poems that he read to boys in order to gain their favor. His own life was quite an adventure: He studied in Carthage, Athens and Rome where he was a lawyer. He then went off to Asia and Egypt to study philosophy and various cults, becoming even a priest of Isis. During his travels he met a very wealthy widow whose hand he won, through magic spells and charms, said her family when they found out they were no longer in her will. Later, he read his works in public and organized gladiatorial events, both of which won him great popularity. At the end of the *Golden Ass* he changed back into a man by eating roses--the well-known antidote for those changed into asses--but was ill received by his lover who had preferred him as an ass with a huge member.

RENT-BOY SEX IN ROME

As seen from the above, Roman men could do as they wished with any non-Roman citizen, be it a boy or a girl. As sex was desirable, Roman men recognized and accepted as normal anything sexual a man could covet sexually. His conscience never troubled him, as is the case in our times, where guilt is an arm used in schools, church and at home. A minimum of discretion was all that was called for.

Prostitution was legally licensed and taxed. The prostitutes were often slaves and non-Romans, lacking in social standing, the most desired of which were often actors and gladiators, the first noted for the salability and attraction since the beginning of recorded history, the second the epitome of masculinity, as are today's athletes. Erotic art in Pompeii and Herculaneum testifies to what was important to the Romans:

Fresco of Priapus from the Casa dei Vettii in Pompeii

Boys found work in taverns and brothels, but were in competition with those who gave it away, even emperors: Stark naked, Elagabalus would stand at the door of his palace or a tavern or the entrance to the baths and offer himself to all comers, out Messalina-ing Messalina. (According to David Bret in his book *Errol Flynn*, Flynn did the same thing, standing nude and fully erected in his studio dressing room, the door open, taking on anyone who would enter, girl or boy.) Elagabalus also had pimps sent to the far corners of the empire to bring him well-endowed boys, sailors being his specialty, for whom he paid vast sums, a column of gold for the length of their chief attribute.

Elagabalus

Born in Syria, he became a priest of the god Elagabal (meaning god of the mountain--El-Gabal, or Baal). In Rome he raised the god higher even than Jupiter. In fact, he returned from Syria with the Black Stone, the most sacred object in the worship of Baal, and built the Elagaballium, a temple on the Palatine to honor it. To the disgust of Romans, cattle and sheep were sacrificed there at the dawn of every day, to please the new sun god, and senators were obliged to attend. During one yearly ceremony in honor of Elagabal he marched backwards, facing pure white horses drawing a chariot, perhaps winking at its driver, the well-known and well-hung Hierocles, a blond athlete he had married and whom he called his husband. The triumphal procession was in homage to the Black Stone's summer residence, outside the city. His second favorite was another athlete, Aurelius Zoticus, who was named Master of the Bedroom and whom he called, according to *Augustan History*, his husband. (The *Augustan History* is a collection of biographies compiled from the works of six different historians.) In honor of his god, Elagabalus had himself circumcised. After his death both the new religion and circumcision died a deserved death (especially the latter, an abominable mutilation unless the boy is old enough to decide, for himself, whether to have it done or not). He married five times, one of his wives being a Vestal Virgin, a flagrant disrespect for Roman law and an action that should have seen the Vestal buried alive and her ravisher put to death. One of his other wives had a husband he ordered killed so they could marry. Herodian claims that he was extremely good looking, and also that he offered his physician ''vast sums of money'' to cut him a cunt--which the doctor sagely declined to do.

He was only called Elagabalus after his death. During his reign he was Marcus Aurelius Antoninus Augustus.

Elagabalus became emperor at age 14, following the assassination of Caracalla, a bloodthirsty murderer responsible for thousands of deaths. While urinating at the roadside, a member of Caracalla's personal guard, Julius Martialis, whose brother Caracalla had had executed a few days before, ran him threw with his sword. Caracalla was 29. Martialis was immediately shot dead by a Scythian archer. Caracalla was replaced by the head of his Imperial Guard, a man Julia Maesa, Elagabalus' vicious grandmother, ordered killed so that Elagabalus could take his place as emperor. As she was wealthy in the extreme, she had bought off all the guards. Julia Maesa's daughter--Elagabalus' mother--helped things along by claiming that she had had an affair with Caracalla, and that Elagabalus was Caracalla's son, making him heir to the throne. Both Julia Maesa and his mother became senators, the first women ever allowed in the senate (and the last). Around the same time that Elagabalus lost Caracalla, on whom it was said he had a huge crush, he lost his father and grandfather, both of whom he seemed to have dearly loved, all of which seemed to have been highly destabilizing for the adolescent boy.

Elagabalus' style of life could only make enemies within the senate and nobility, and disgust among Romans in general. His grandmother, the same who had put him on the throne, realizing her mistake in having him named emperor, conspired with her *second* daughter to have *her* son, Alexander Severus, age 13, replace Elagabalus. Elagabalus didn't know the details of the conspiracy but he did know that something was up and that Alexander was involved. As the bad blood between them became known, they were both summoned to the headquarters of the Imperial Guard in hopes that a solution could be found. Elagabalus, believing he still had the backing of his grandmother and of her wealth, accepted to appear before the guard with Alexander. He did so accompanied by his mother. On arrival the guards cheered Alexander, and Elagabalus, vexed, ordered the immediate execution of Alexander's followers. In response, the guard stripped both Elagabalus and his mother naked, decapitated them, dragged the remains through Rome and threw what was left into the Tiber. Elagabalus was 18.

Later, Alexander was himself killed by his guard at age 27 when he tried to buy off the German enemy instead of fighting them bravely as a Roman should.

In Greece boys met in oil shops and perfume stalls, in Rome barbershops were preferred, as well as the baths, naturally, and outside cruising fields, such as barracks, alleys, arcades surrounding the market (known as ''*fornices*'' from which we have our word fornication) and gymnasiums. The boys often gave it away until they became aware of their value, selling themselves afterwards. Brothels were not noted for their cleanliness and sexual acts were subtly lighted by burning lamps, which accounts for Seneca's remark: ''You reek still of the soot of the brothel.''

In Rome rent boys had their own festival, the Robigalia, in honor of a god that infected agriculture with diseases, but if propitiated would save crops. On the day of the festival there were chariot races and the sacrifice of a dog. Because male prostitution was taxed, Cato said that it brought in more money than farming. The celebration of rent boys may have just fallen on the day of the Robigalia, and had nothing directly to do with it.

Christianity and later religions destroyed free sexuality from Byzantine times to our own, when homosexuality was first punished with death. As we will see throughout this book, this did not stop some popes from being atheists, others from making cardinals out of their rent boys, still others from incest--up to our own times when thousands and thousands of boys have been sexually abused by priests and other scum-dwelling leeches that have handicapped men mentally as surely as if they had been lobotomized. And as witnessed in nearly monthly televised beheadings, religious obscurantism still has a bright future ahead of it.

Of course, the needs of a man's stomach and scrotum are such that he is pragmatic in his ability to juggle what is divine and what is profane, all the while to his advantage, and *enlightened* men then and today have followed and will always follow the "road less traveled by", and lead their own lives in their own way, dissimilating, lying and cheating when necessary, like Galileo who had to disown the heresy of the Earth encircling the sun. It is the reason why in the film industry, as well as nearly everywhere else, what the French call *mariages blancs* are *still* practiced, and why Brad Davis had to hide his fatal illness to keep feeding his family. In several countries a lad can now marry the boy of his dreams, but he would nonetheless be crazy (or insanely courageous) to admit to his locker-room buddies that he prefers them to the chirping maidens in the showers next door.

SATYRICON

Petronius (27-66 A.D.), the author of the *Satyricon*, wrote that at age 14 he was Nero's favorite, offering himself to both Nero and his wife, in exchange for wealth and position. Tacitus, Plutarch and Pliny the Elder say that Petronius was the palace arbiter of elegance during Nero's reign. Later he became a senator. He reportedly slept during the day and spent his night in work and orgies, the organization of which placed him in the spheres of genius. His closeness to Nero attracted jealousy, ending with the commander of the Imperial Guard accusing him of treason. As he had lived his entire life in the way he wished to live it, he decided to do the same with his death. He opened his veins amidst a group of friends, and during their conversation he bandaged them or opened them again according to his whims, discussing only light subjects, poetry and verses. He dined. He offered gifts. He even slept before beginning a new round of entertainment. He did finally weaken and die, in his mid-forties. He left a special present for Nero, his will in which he described in detail the emperor's debauchery and the name of the men who had participated in his bacchanals. He then broke his signet ring so that Nero couldn't use it on documents the emperor would employ to kill his enemies, pretending that they were accusatory confessions from Petronius himself.

Nero's court was founded on immorality, extravagance and making money, at which Petronius' talent was paramount. Perhaps a tenth of his *Satyricon* is left. It seems crass to some, perhaps because of the male-male sex, but to the Romans there wasn't the slightest reason for scandal. The manuscript was found around 1450 in Renaissance Milan, then lost again, and found in Padua in the mid-1650s. What we would consider the dirty parts may have been expunged by Monks, but we can't be sure. It was certainly based on real people and consisted of a trio, Encolpius, meaning something like ''he who embraces cock,'' his former lover Ascylotos, ''he who can do it all night,'' who badly wanted Encolpius' new boy, Giton, ''neighbor.'' Only one dirty part remains, this one: ''When he finished reciting, he came to kiss me and then climbed on my couch and pulled away my clothes. I resisted, but in vain. He manipulated my member which refused to engorge.'' In the first part of the book Encolpius had done something to anger Priapus, the result of which accounts for his impotence.

The book opens with the three going to a place near Naples, calling themselves teachers and taking in gullible Romans on the way. They have adventures with pimps, rapists and rent boys. The climax comes when Encolpius discovers Giton making mad love with another boy and beats him.

In a following fragment, *à la Keystone Cops*, the three have stolen some money that they hide in the lining of a coat that is then stolen by someone else. They find the coat but are nearly arrested for another coat they'd stolen, although they finally make off with the original coat with the money still intact.

Another fragment informs us that a statue of Priapus with a huge dick was placed in gardens to assure the fertility of the plants there. In trying to steal the statue Encoplius brings impotence down on himself (the natural result of showing Priapus disrespect). Then comes a fragment called the Dinner with Trimalchio, probably Nero himself, the purpose of which is to impress the guests with the incredible cost of the feast. Along the line we also learn that crucified Christians were not given burial, thereby denying them an afterlife.

There's a side fragment involving a poet, Eumolpus, who tells the story of his life to a young boy whom he succeeds in seducing.

In the final scene they go to Croton (the very south of Italy) where men specialize in legacy hunting. Eumolpus, the poet, plays the role of a rich patron, causing a feeding frenzy by those who want to be his legatee. He stages his own funeral and in his will he leaves all to he who will eat his cadaver. The book ends with one and all finding comical justification for the cannibalism they're getting ready to commit.

The purpose of the book is to entertain. There's no moral. No morality.

RENAISSANCE

SCIPIONE BORGHESE
1445 - 1510

The hagiography of Sebastian falls invitingly into the story of Renaissance painters and sculptors as his burial place, San Sebastiano fuori le mura, was rebuilt by Scipione Borghese around 1610, at the time of the death of Caravaggio. The importance of Scipione Borghese to us is the combination of several factors: Born Scipione Caffarelli he was turned over to Camillo Borghese, the future Pope Paul V, because his father, fallen on hard times, didn't have the funds to educated and bring him up in a noble manner. Paul V changed the boy's name to Borghese and made him a cardinal and his secretary. Scipione guarded the door to the pope, thanks to which he amassed an immense fortune, making him perhaps the wealthiest man in Rome. (His ''salary'' alone, for 1612, was 140,000 scudi, while François I offered Cellini a yearly stipend of 300 scudi, which gives one an idea of what Scipione was worth.) To these factors were added his gift of extreme intelligence and passion for art and the collection of art, turning the Palazzo Borghese into an incomparable museum, while assuring the material comfort of Caravaggio and Bernini, among others.

Scipione Borghese

Against Paul V's wishes, Scipione brought his lover Stephen Pignatelli to Rome and together they filled the palazzo Borghese with homoerotic art. Pignatelli was said to have loved Scipione to the point of insanity. Both men shared the services of other boys they paid, one of whom, age 18, they were thought to have ordered murdered, just outside their bedroom, perhaps because the boy had sought bribes to keep Scipione's tendencies from his uncle the pope. Pignatelli was requested to leave Rome but was brought back when Scipione became deathly ill, and only his lover's presence could heal him. Scipione immediately recovered and was awarded a cardinal's hat.

Scipione commissioned Bernini to sculpt a Hermaphrodite, a reclining figure with an ample appendage, found today in the Louvre, the backside to the public. In order to view the statue's singularity, one has to squeeze between the pedestal (and wonderfully sculpted mattress over which the Hermaphrodite reclines) and a wall, which only people who know what to look for do (at least that was the logistics a number of years ago when I viewed it).

Paul awarded Scipione 105 paintings confiscated from the artist Cavaliere d'Arpino to cover unpaid taxes, among which were the *Sick Bacchus* and *A Boy with a Basket* by Caravaggio. Caravaggio had worked for Cavaliere d'Arpino as an apprentice, churning out paintings of fruit and flowers.

The pope also stole Raphael's *The Deposition* from the Baglioni Chapel in Perugia, gave it to Scipione, and then legalized the theft with something called the *motu proprio* which somehow made what a pope did lawful.

JULIUS III
1487 – 1555

Julius III replaced Paul III. He was a lucky pope in that during his reign Queen Mary returned to the English throne and Catholicism was restored in England, all of which led to his glorification and allowed him to live the lazy, dissolute existence he favored. Added to this was the fact that he possessed great administrative talent and as he had been named governor of Rome twice, he had that center too in his corner. He built an incredibly luxurious palace, the Villa Giolia, adorned by Michelangelo, Vasari and lesser artists who decorated it with Ganymedes and other soft-core pornographic satyrs and naked angels--for which he emptied the papal treasury.

Like da Vinci and his Salaì, Julius had fulfilled his erotic fantasies thanks to a youngster, Santino, a streetwise rent boy of 14 he saw and lusted for. He had his brother adopt the lad who then became his nephew, on whom he showered benefices and named a cardinal, ennobled under the title of Innocenzo Ciocchi del Monte. He boasted of the boy's prowess in bed, Julius being the bottom to "his hung boy."

Of Julius the governor of Milan wrote, "They say many bad things about this pope, that he is vicious, arrogant and crazy." Thomas Beard wrote: "He makes a cardinal only of those who bugger him." The Venetian ambassador to the Vatican, Matteo Dandolo, wrote home to say that "the pope shared his bed with a boy cardinal." Cardinal Jean du Bellay wrote a sonnet about Santino, the pope's catamite "with the red hat of a cardinal on his head," and the pope's entourage complained that Julius didn't have a head for business while impatiently awaiting the boy as one does one's mistress.

After the pope's death Innocenzo killed two men who had insulted him in some unrecorded way. The newly elected Pope Pius IV had him arrested and imprisoned for several years. He was again arraigned for raping two women but was released thanks to Julius' friends. Innocenzo died in obscurity and was buried, without a funeral, in the del Monte chapel next to his benefactor who had preceded him in death at age 68, from fever.

A virgin by birth (the 10th September), Julius III's full name was Giovanni Maria Ciocchi del Monte. Raised in Rome and given a humanist education, he was present during the Sack of Rome. Julius was handed over to Charles V as a hostage in order for Clement VII to be able to leave the fortress of Sant'Angelo.

His election as pope took ten weeks, one of the longest in papal history. Sources say that during this time not only did the air in the Vatican become more fetid because the cardinals were literally walled in, but their usual meeting place for secret negotiations, the latrines, stunk so badly that they were hardly approachable. In addition, the food supply was lessened and made coarser in an attempt to encourage a result. The cardinals were split in factions, and del Monte turned out to be the least offensive candidate, a perfect choice in that he did nothing to rock the boat politically.

Once elected he spent his time in supervising the building of his villa, in hunting, in banquets and the theater. Only his known preference for rent boys caused a stir, a scandal that was welcome fodder for Protestants.

CENCI MURDER
1598 - 1599

Even a terrible flood that left 1,500 dead couldn't keep all Rome from being stunned by a murder among the nobility, that of Count Francesco Cenci by his coachman--his daughter's lover--Calvetti, who bludgeoned him with a hammer. The count had at first been drugged by his daughter, Beatrice, assisted by her stepmother, the count's wife Lucrezia, whom Count Cenci repeatedly raped in front of Beatrice. Count Cenci had been ruined by a fine of 100,000 *scudi* for sodomizing his stable boys, as the most exciting rent boys have traditionally been stable hands. His sons, Giacomo and Bernardo, were in on the plot, as the count had tried to sodomize them too, as well as having incest with Beatrice. (She's thought to have had a child, but from her father or the coachman is unknown.) The murder was camouflaged as an accident by shoving the count's body over the broken railing of his palazzo. It was the murder of the century and even Pope Clement wanted to be kept continually up-to-date. If this weren't enough, a Cenci cousin, Paolo di Santa Croce, killed his mother when she refused to bequeath him her estate. The pope could understand murder to ensure one's inheritance. What he wanted were details concerning Cenci. He knew the Cenci were part of Rome's most ancient aristocracy. Cristoforo Cenci had worked for the Papal court and had amassed a fortune in mansions, farms and palaces, all of which he left to his son Francesco at his death, when the boy was twelve. His mother couldn't control her son who attacked servants at the slightest provocation, shedding blood and accumulating lawsuits. Even at age twelve he tried to bend male and female servants and stable boys to his sexual will, and contented himself, his hand always down his trousers, when the palace help--and courtesans that he was already frequenting--were unavailable. His mother married him off at age fourteen to a girl the same age. His own children soon followed, among whom were Giacomo, Cristoforo, Rocco, Bernardo and Beatrice.

His sexual attacks on the palace servants continued, with his being forced to pay up when he lost suits, although on one occasion he was able to get a boy hung thanks to false witnesses in his pay. Accusations against him were usually based on brutality, fornication and sodomy. On occasion he was imprisoned, earning his freedom only by shelling out what amounted to tens of thousands of scudi. A period of instability followed when one dead pope was replaced by another in rapid succession. Criminality and debauchery reigned supreme, a perfect climate for Cenci whose physical and sexual violence continued unchecked.

His wife died in childbirth and he took another, Lucrezia, whom he raped when she was unwilling to have sex, rapes that took place in front of his daughter Beatrice, all the while continuing to sodomize his stable hands. His sons Giacomo and Bernardo became aware of their father's attacks on boys, and finally Cenci was brought to trial for sodomy and found guilty. By paying 100,000 scudi, a colossal sum, to the Papal Exchequer, he escaped being burned at the stake.

Cristoforo and Rocco, following in their father's steps, were both killed in duels over whores, and Cenci retired to a mountain palace retreat accessible with difficulty even by mule with Lucrezia and Beatrice. The palace retreat was looked after by an extremely handsome caretaker, Olympio Calvetti, who became Beatrice's lover. Cenci returned to Rome, leaving the two women virtual prisoners. When he returned it was to continue the rape of his wife and his daughter.

Finally Beatrice convinced her stepmother and her lover Calvetti to rid them all of Cenci. Calvetti enlisted the help of a friend, Marzio Catalano, and together they entered Cenci's bedroom and bludgeoned the sleeping figure to death. Cenci was then pushed from the palace balcony. The protective balustrade was later broken so as to appear an accident.

Cenci's sons, Giocomo and Bernardo, returned from Rome, although neither they nor Lucrezia and Beatrice took part in Cenci's burial, which got people talking to such an extent that an enquiry was made. Calvetti's wife, jealous that her husband had had a child with Beatrice (unless it was her father's) told the investigators that she had seen her husband destroy the balustrade *after* Cenci had fallen. Marzio, too, soon admitted his role in the affair. It came out that Giocomo, in Rome, had known about the assassination plans, but Bernardo had not.

Cenci's body was exhumed and it was found that his ghastly wounds could not have been caused by a simple fall.

At the trial the people of Rome were in favor of Beatrice when the details of her ordeal came out, and Giacomo and Bernardo testified that Cenci had tried to sodomize them. But the pope and the nobility had no desire whatsoever to see any of them escape punishment, as that would open the doors for their own assassination at the hands of disgruntled children and servants.

Lucrezia and Beatrice were accompanied by so many thousands to their place of execution, all wailing the coming death of the two martyrs, that segments of the crowd fell into the Tiber and were drowned. Both were beheaded. Giacomo and Calvetti were paraded through the streets while red-hot pinchers pulled flesh from their bodies. At the execution site both were bludgeoned to death, their bodies cut into pieces, and hung on hooks

Innocent little Bernardo was informed that he would suffer the same fate. He was obliged to witness the executions of all four before being told he would only be obliged to man the pope's galleys until his death, which those in the know knew to be worse than death itself. The pope was given the details, and declared himself satisfied.

Beatrice by Reni

CARLO GESUALDO
1560 – 1613

During an October night at the Palazzo San Serero in Naples, 1590, servants heard screams for help, followed by gunshots. They knew the mistress of the palace, Maria d'Avalos, was entertaining the most handsome man of the late Renaissance, Fabrizio Carafa, Duke of Andria, while her husband Gesualdo was supposedly off hunting. Either he had returned early fortuitously or he had finally heard what everyone else had known for two years, that his wife, the daughter of the Marquis of Pescara and the niece of Pope Pius IV, was carrying on a love affaire. Aided by friends, Gesualdo come across the nude couple in the spacious bedroom. He thrust his sword through Fabrizio before stabbing Maria, paralyzed, screaming, nearby. He then returned to Fabrizio's body and repeatedly harpooned it with such force that holes were made in the marble flooring. He left the room covered with blood, but was called back, perhaps by groans. Declaring, "They're still alive!" he turned his hunting arm on Fabrizio and shot him through the side, the bullet entering the elbow and plunging into the chest, followed by the coup de grâce, a bullet in the head, splattering both Fabrizio and himself. He went to his wife, still breathing, and slit her throat from ear to ear. He then took his knife to Fabrizio's sexual attributes, emasculating the boy, before turning the weapon on his wife and hacking at the source of her infidelity. Historians claim that at the time, murder was a noble's only means of revenge, as were duels when one's nonsexual honor was at stake.

In his rage he went to his youngest son's rooms and, dagger in hand, ended the boy's life, as Gesualdo had convinced himself that the child's eyes were not his own. Years later he would end the life of his oldest son, for unknown reasons, his sword plunged into the lad's chest. He would marry again, Eleonora d'Este of Ferrara, threaten her, take the life of the boy she gave him, his third son, and meet his own death immediately afterwards, at the hands of Eleonora--a dagger to the neck as he slept--who knew it was her only means of survival.

A sadomasochist, it's unknown if his sadomasochism began before the Palazzo San Serero massacre or was a result of it. He himself had been unfaithful, finding sexual release with rent boys, eventually allowing himself to be flagellated by them.

Gesualdo was a recognized musician who had written six books on madrigals and three on sacred works. He was an accomplished player of the guitar, the lute and the harpsichord, although some critics wonder if his talent was real or a byproduct of the reputation he gained as a murderer. It is known, however, that Stravinsky was influenced by his oeuvre.

He suffered from depression but, again, whether before or as a result of the killings is a mystery. It is known however that he sought treatment of sorts by attempting to obtain relics from the body of his uncle, a cardinal who later became Saint Borromeo, relics valued for their curative purposes--without success as the church refused to turn them over.

He also consorted with witches, two of which his second wife had had condemned by a tribunal, but in the same way that his nobility had been the reason why he had escaped punishment for his murders--*and* the fact that he was the wealthiest man in Naples--he was able to have them imprisoned in his own palace, where he had sexual access to both.

Because the following details were recorded during the trial of the two witches and are therefore authentic (which is very rare for events dating back 400 years), I'll grudgingly include them: To heal Gesualdo from his depression and other ills, the witches had him impregnate them while they were menstruating. Bread was then stuffed into the vagina that he then consumed. Sorry.

Gesualdo

ROMANTIC TIMES

THOMAS BECKFORD
1760 - 1844

Of Thomas Beckford the author Alistair Sutherland wrote: He was ''as much a martyr as Wilde, and almost certainly a more interesting and civilized man.'' And that's exactly the problem. The more one reads about Beckford the more one wants to know about his intellectual inner life. One feels the wondrous potential in the man through his books, his essays, travels logs, architectural constructions and satires, making him one of the most fascinating men in this book. Cellini in his autobiography made us feel the intense love he felt for his boys, and when he described how he and a lad suddenly found themselves at the gates leading out of Florence, and just as suddenly decided to follow the yellow-brick-road of adventure to Rome, one's heart leaps at the thrill of these two lovers off to discover the world. We know nothing of this kind concerning Beckford. It's a huge pity because one intensely feels that Beckford intensely felt, and it is certain that he was intellectually and poetically capable of the sublime, the sublime being, for me, this: ''What is everything that men have thought and done over the centuries compared with just one moment of love?'' (Friedrich Hölderlin). He also took wondrous care of the boys he kept.

If this painting of Beckford is realistic,
his lovers were fortunate.

The origin of the family fortune went back to buccaneers who established themselves in Jamaica, founded plantations of sugar cane worked by slaves, horrendous work, under a blazing sun, cutting the cane with machetes after burning the fields to free them of cane leaves and insects, many of which, especially the centipedes, nonetheless survived the fires (I know because I myself spent two years teaching on Jamaica). The first Beckfords were violent men with uncontrollable tempers, and the boy we're concerned with would be as irascible. Each generation of Beckfords produced dozens of children, and William's father was said to have had thirty, although William was the only legitimate heir. When a friend told his father that he was sending his son to Richmond, Beckford senior said he wouldn't because the air was bad, proof being that twelve of his children had died just after birth there. Beckford senior had taken up residence in England where he was educated at Oxford, eventually becoming Lord Mayor of London. He died when William was nine, but his force of character ruled the boy's life until his own death, many years later. William's father was a commoner and his mother, Maria, a Hamilton, thought she had married below her, as she could trace her lineage back to James II of Scotland and Edward III of England. She resembled her husband only in her strength of will and determination, and while he was a free thinker, she was a strict Calvinist.

As desired as Henry VIII's boy, as longed for as the son Giovanni worshipped, the monumental artist Cellini, William was raised with supreme care and in luxury. The boy was said to have been immediately aware of his wealth and worth.

He grew up in a mansion of deep red fabrics and wall coverings, with gold cornices. The lands surrounding the mansion were gardens that gave on to wild woods of deer and undulating hills. The boy's father wanted to construct a tower that he did not live long enough to realize, but his son would fulfill his dreams in spades. William grew up alongside a sister, his mother's daughter from a previous marriage, but she was too old for them to ever become close, although he wrote to her constantly. When his father died a friend wrote of him: He was too good to make a Devil but too Turbulent for an Angel. He was one to ride Whirlwinds and direct Storms.

Brian Fothergill, in his wonderful book *Beckford of Fonthill*, wrote that the child filled his boyhood with dreams of the woods being inhabited by knights, gods and heroes, created by his fertile imagination.

His father's wish to make certain that his bastards received their just part of the inheritance reduced the sum that came down to Beckford. The boy himself cared nothing for the details of his worth, interested as he was in the profits. But for the solitary lad, the loss of the father he genuinely loved and admired was a tragedy. He found himself more alone than ever, in a household run by women.

For every favorable commentary concerning Beckford there is an equal and opposite criticism. Around his property he constructed a 12-foot-high wall. Those who favor him claim that it was to protect foxes from ruthless hunters, while others say it was to conceal the orgies that took place within his boy houri. Slaves worked his plantations in Jamaica and he saw nothing wrong in possessing them as he possessed his boys, in exchange--in the case of the boys--for money. He set sail for Jamaica at age 21 but for reasons unknown (some say sea sickness, others filth aboard the ships in an era where sanitation was nonexistent) he disembarked in Portugal where he had multiple liaisons with Portuguese boys whose nonchalant sexuality he highly favored, and where he made the acquaintance of Gregorio Franchi, a beautiful choir boy, at first a sex object, then his pimp, to whom we'll return in a moment. He had a dwarf whose task was to open the 38-foot-high doors to his palace, which he called his Abbey, dedicated to his personal patron saint, St. Nicholas. The reason behind employing the dwarf was to make the doors seem even higher, said his critics, although his friends claimed that Beckford had saved the dwarf--whom he had seen, in Italy, being beaten to death by his father because of the poor devil's misshapen form--offering him a place at his side for life. Beckford lived to age 84 because he took care of himself, watching over what he ate, and turning in early every night. But his detractors maintained he was no more than a hypochondriac, a *Malade Imaginaire*. His every day, when old, consisted of riding through his properties before breakfast, during which he stopped at the homes of the poor, coming to their aid should they not be able to help themselves; then came reading until noon, business with those who oversaw his fortune, another ride for exercise, more visits to his lands to supervise plantings and constructions, a late afternoon dinner followed by the study of catalogues concerning future acquisitions, especially books--both undertakings he adored--more reading and early to bed. His enemies evoke non-stop orgies of boys among themselves, the old man looking on and taking what pleasure was left to him.

    This is naturally in contrast to younger years. He states that his parents saw he received a thorough education under competent tutors, especially Dr. Lettice, age 34, and William Chambers, who assured a solid grounding in Latin and Greek, Persian, Italian, German, French and Portuguese, as well as philosophy, law and physics. During a visit to a close friend of his father's, he entertained the man with a speech he had memorized, from Thucydides, that he had himself translated from the Greek. Robert Drysdale, age 27, was another tutor who called Beckford's residence, Fonthill, a palace, and remained with Beckford for four years. Beckford was curious and his thirst for knowledge inextinguishable. He was not allowed companions his own age due to his mother's fear of moral contamination, perhaps a partial reason for his violent temper and outbursts, although they were part and parcel of his heritage from the first Beckford buccaneers. ''I was living amidst a fine collection of art, under competent tutors. I was studious and diligent from inclination.'' His first book, written at age 17, was *Vathek*, still in print. The twists and turns of *Vathek* make *Lord of the Rings* simplicity itself: revolts, orgies, effeminate lovers, descent into Hell, spells, supernatural powers, talismans, the sacrifice of 50 children, religious renunciation, dwarves galore, towers galore, torture, genies, lascivious dances, beautiful young men, wondrous girls, eternal youth, viziers and eunuchs, and finally eternal damnation, which is a respite from all the above, the whole written in one sitting over three days and two nights, Beckford tells us. Byron used one of the book's characters in a poem, and the book is said on a par with the poet Shelley's wife's *Frankenstein*. Keats *Endymion* is based in part on *Vathek* and it inspired two works by Lovecraft and poems by Mallarmé.

He was also tutored in art by Alexander Cozens, and in music by Mozart himself (whose father made certain his son was there where there was money to earn). Mozart was 9, Beckford 6. They met later in Vienna where Beckford found him strange and melancholic, ''but more wonderful than ever''. (It must be added that there is no proof of their ever having met and Mozart's father, who kept a detailed diary, never mentions such an encounter.)

Alexander Cozens was a Russian steeped in mystery, a teacher at Eton, who was said to have been Peter the Great's bastard. He encouraged Beckford's interest in the Orient, mythology, knights and chivalry, and perhaps sparked his interests in magic, an interest he would have throughout his life, and it was perhaps Cozens too who was the first to unlock the door to sexual secrets. Under his influence Beckford began writing about glens and fawns and grottos, and especially about mysterious towers.

Thanks to the family library he discovered treasures like the *Arabian Nights,* although his mother had ordered it kept out of his hands, a book that may have sparked an early sexuality. We know of his love for William Courtenay, called Kitty by family and friends, the only boy of 14 children. Kitty was 3rd Viscount until he later petitioned to revive the title of 9th Earl of Devon. Said to have been the most beautiful boy in England, he was also thought to have been Beckford's lover when he was age 10, to Beckford's 18. De Vinci's Salaì was 10 too, and Cellini had lovers of that age. In Florence during the time of Lorenzo de' Medici boys aged 9 and over sold themselves, so there was nothing unusual about the fact. The problem was that the penalty for sodomy in England at the time was the pillory and/or death. (The pillory is explained and illustrated elsewhere.) The *Arabian Nights*, for those of you who have forgotten your college course in The-Correct-use-of-Virgins 101, was hardly a child's tale. A sultan, tired of his wives' infidelities, decided to marry a succession of virgins that he would ''honor'' and then execute, the ultimate guarantee of their fidelity. One of the maidens was Scheherazade who began a tale on the night of their wedding but failed to finish it. As the Sultan wanted to know the end, he suspended her death for 1,001 nights. The tales certainly inspired Beckford because his book *Vathek* is set in an Arabian context, with ghouls, sorcerers and magicians similar to those found in the *Arabian Nights*, as well as erotic passages.

His education was continued in Geneva at the University where he was accompanied by Lettice. He met Voltaire, 84, and he deeply appreciated the mountains which enhanced his love for wildlife and animals, a love he had had from boyhood. His mother had chosen Geneva as a Calvinist refuge from heathenism but it was there, at age 17, that he met and loved his first boy, which the author Fothergill assures us was quite normal, as all over Europe, in every boarding school, boys were engaged in sexual adventures. As Beckford put everything on paper, including, in reference to the boy he loved, ''whose dark eyes drank eager draughts of pleasure from my sight'', word got out to his mother who ordered him home. But he had learned a lot in Geneva, perfecting his Italian, Spanish and Portuguese, and starting Arabic.

In 1780 he went on the Grand Tour, an obligation for aristocratic boys, and a chance to educate himself because, as you'll learn in the life of Byron, Oxford and Cambridge were known for little more, at the time, than a place where boys met and ''did'' other boys. So the Grand Tour was a window onto the outer world, as echoed by Dr. Johnson who said it perfectly: ''A man who has not been to Italy is conscious of an inferiority, from his not having seen what is expected a man should see.'' His companion was here too Lettice.

In Venice he met a countess, her husband, two daughters and son. One of the girls fell in love with him and when she declared herself he told her straight out that it was her brother, Cornaro, he wanted. She took poison, taking care that the dosage wasn't lethal.

He visited Florence where he went mad over the galleries he visited, with their paintings, statuary and bronze busts, a romantic young man's candy store.

At Luca he attended a concert where the star was a castrati, the successor to the great Farinelli. He appreciated the boy so much that he wrote, concerning him, ''My blood thrills in my veins.'' From there on he would have a great attachment for castrati, that he had the financial means of fulfilling.

Beckford was an Olympic champion letter writer and wrote mostly to his sister to whom he could not admit his intimate feelings, and certainly not any sexual experiences he may have had. When he returned to Fonthill he found a strange letter awaiting him from a woman who knew, about the boy he loved in Venice, Cornaro, telling him to forget the past, ''for Heaven's sake keep a perpetual watch over yourself or you will be a lost man." Nature, continued the letter, had lavished so many talents on him that he must always be on his guard. "If not, your reputation will be lost forever, lost *never never* to be regained." Perhaps something physical took place between the two boys, but at any rate the ending of the letter would prove true, his reputation would be lost, never ever to be regained.

Just after receiving the letter he turned 21 and took possession of Fonthill, in the company of Kitty and his teacher Cozens. A three-day orgy ensued, involving musicians and youths of both sexes, following which he entered on the most prolific period of his life. He began his book *Vathek*, in which Caliph Vathek built a tower "from an insolent curiosity of penetrating the secrets of Heaven." And in a letter he wrote, to a friend, "I am growing rich and mean to build Towers." "My Arabian tales go on prodigiously", he wrote to another. He put other letters together for his book on his Grand Tour. He composed music and an operetta. Young, handsome and filthy rich, London society opened to him and he literally danced the nights away, seldom leaving a salon before six in the morning. "All London," he wrote, "is at my feet and all the Misses in array whenever I show myself." When he traveled he ordered innkeepers to decorate rooms to his taste before his arrival. He was painted by Joshua Reynolds and wrote Cozens that he "had reveled till ten in the morning" with Kitty. On the road he wrote to Kitty, "I read your letter with a beating heart and kissed it a thousand times. I would sacrifice every drop of blood in my veins to do you good."

To allay rumors of misbehavior, it was decided that he marry, a common occurrence for homosexuals--Wilde had married twice--but Beckford was heterosexually operative, and had certainly, by then, discovered pleasures offered by females--perhaps even early, with a girl he corresponded with over the years and who adored him, Louise Beckford, wife of his cousin Peter, six years older than he. He chose Lady Margaret Gordon, a woman he sincerely appreciated, a wife with a personality of her own but one who gladly left the spotlight to him. She was soon pregnant. He entered politics, an area we won't enter as Beckford did so only because it was expected of his caste. His interest in Kitty--a lad who was now 16, effeminate, one the author of *Beckford of Fonthill* describes as being "shallow" and "worthless"--decreased in the Greek sense that the boy had outgrown his role as a hairless depository of virile male semen. But England being England, the lad's effeminacy would be appreciated by others for years to come.

Margaret gave birth to a son born dead, Beckford's greatest tragedy since the death of his father. But she was soon again pregnant.

In the meantime Beckford faced the greatest threat to his life. He had a gift for imitating people, one he used to amuse his friends. One victim was Lord Loughborough, who didn't appreciate Beckford's mimicry.

Loughborough became an enemy. He married Kitty's sister and immediately became aware of the affection that existed between his young nephew and the rake Beckford. At the time Kitty had been 13, Beckford 18, and it would indeed have been difficult for a lord to accept the image of his sister's baby brother being fucked at such a tender age by a rich, loud-mouthed, disrespectful adolescent who mimicked him behind his back.

His revenge took years but his plans to discover Kitty and Beckford in Love's sweet embrace paid off. There were various versions of what happened next. In one version the activity between the two, extremely boisterous one afternoon, alerted a servant who alerted Courtenay's uncle who revealed the scandal to the press. Or, some say, the uncle intercepted love letters between the two and then contacted the press, which seems more logical than having been turned in by Kitty's servants because the servants must have been used to the goings on in the manor since Kitty's puberty. Still another author has one of his tutors spying on the couple, through the bedroom keyhole, in full intercourse. All of this may have been the reason for the future wall around Fonthill and the creation of an inner spy-free sanctum. The reality is that Loughborough had planned the whole denouement. Why all of this hadn't been disposed of in private is unknown, although, perhaps, Courtenay had refused to stop ''seeing'' Beckford when ordered by his uncle to do so, leaving the uncle little choice other than going public.

Beckford's wife's young brother came to save his sister who was now apprised of what had happened. Described as fiery and furious, he caught Beckford by the lapels of his gown and slapped him, thereby hoping to force him into a duel. Beckford resisted the temptation and the brother, whose sister remained loyal to Beckford, could do nothing more than ride away.

Back home Kitty confessed all and surrendered Beckford's letters to Loughborough, alas lost today, but leaving no doubt to their liaison. Beckford called a meeting at Fonthill, attended by Lettice and his mother, both aware of his bisexuality, his wife and a family friend, Lord Thurlow, known for his judicious advice. Beckford was told that the law demanded death for sodomy, and that even if he were found not guilty, his reputation would be compromised forever should the case go to court.

Incredibly, his mother suggested that he go to London and, in effect, plough as many bellies as possible, making the acts as public as possible, so as to enhance his reputation as a womanizer. Lettice and Thurlow suggested he go abroad, the time for the scandal to cool down, the time necessary to negotiate with Lord Loughborough. Beckford went as far as Dover before turning back, decided to face the music.

He faced social ostracism for an entire year before finally exiling himself. He stayed abroad for 10 years, mostly in Portugal, and then Paris where he collected books during the day and boys during the night.

At one point during his exile Beckford snuck back to Fonthill where he was persuaded to visit his estates in Jamaica, as mentioned, by the new master of Fonthill, the man named by Beckford's father to look after his wealth, Thomas Wildman, who had been swindling the boy since his father's death and wished to continue doing so. He convinced the lad that the climate in England was still far to hostel for him to remain. Beckford agreed to go to Jamaica where Wildman's brother, as great a crook, awaited him. In fact, Wildman would manage to hang on for another twenty years. Beckford took a ship bound for Jamaica but at a layover in Lisbon he decided to remain for a week, a sojourn that would last a year and would introduce him to the country he would love as much as his dear Fonthill, and that until his death. He met the Marquis of Marialva who was bowled over by the fascinating lad. Beckford was bowled over by the Marquis' 13-year-old son Dom Pedro, confiding to his diary, ''He loves me, I have tasted the sweetness of his lips.'' At the same time, he became enamored of a 17-year-old choir boy, Gregorio Fellipe Franchi, whom he seduced and who would remain by his side, at first his lover, then in his service. Franchi was amusing, cheerful, and totally devoted to Beckford, and that to his last day. Dom Pedro's father had no idea of what was going on between the two boys, and even delighted in seeing them dance together, something that would have shocked the English, but the Marquis chalked it up to youthful high spirits. Then a friend of the Marquis' saw what was taking place and warned Beckford, in private, of the dire consequence. Following what had happened in England, Beckford listened.

He withdrew from Lisbon and went to Spain where new adventures awaited him, the 14-year-old husband (!) of a Duc's daughter; the 20-year-old son of an ambassador, Prince de Carency; the 22-year-old ambassador to Tripoli and his 12-year-old brother, among others, the sexual outcome of which he did not confide to his diary. Franchi caught up with him in Madrid, armed with a letter from his father confiding the boy into Beckford's care. Truly, the sun was beginning to shine anew in Beckford's life.

Kitty

Courtenay had fled abroad too. He went to America where he had property at Claremont on the Hudson River in N.Y., and then Paris, at his Chateau Dreveil, where he died at age 67, loved, it was said, by his tenants. He was buried in the family homestead in Powderham. We can only hope that during this time he found a virile lad to care for his needs, as Kitty was more than financially able to care for the lad's.

Powderham, Kitty's pad.

Beckford was in Paris too--we don't know if they saw each other but it's highly likely they did if Kitty had been there at the time. The French Revolution was taking place, offering Beckford an occasion to buy up the guillotined aristocrats' possessions.

Beckford's wife died giving him his second daughter. He had truly loved her and "he knew in his heart that the loss was irreparable, that never again would the circumstances of his life present him with a similar chance to restore the wreckage and damage which fate had brought on him, or again offer him the vision of a happier and more reasonable future," wrote Brian Fothergill in *Beckford of Fonthill*. Both girls were farmed out to relatives. His hatred for Loughborough was complete when he publicly held Beckford responsible for her death, saying she had died of a broken heart.

At age 20 Beckford had written a satire *Memoirs of Extraordinary Painters*. The book had begun as a spoof: A household servant had been given the assignment of showing the mansion's paintings to visitors. To help her out, Beckford, then age 17, gave her an *aide-mémoire* from which she read, giving the paintings ridiculous backgrounds, asserting that a painting by Rubens was by Og of Basan, a Murillo was by Blunderbussiana of Venice, another by Herr Sucrewasser and still another by Watersouchy of Vienna, during which time Beckford was in hiding behind curtains, dying of laughter. This is all highly engaging, meaning, perhaps, that to know him was to love him. Among his paintings were some by Titian, Velasquez, Rembrandt and Canaletto.

One commentary on Beckford's life made me smile. The writer regretted the man that Beckford could have become--with all his immense intelligence, creativity and wealth--had he not given himself up to the futilities that marked his life. For me it is just the opposite. It's the road he chose that makes me burst with admiration. There are an incredible number of Englishmen who have done extraordinary things with extraordinary talent and intelligence. Lawrence brought Feisal to Damascus by the force of his will, the explorer Burton spoke 29 languages, Stanley went through a hell impossible to imagine to find Livingston, which in itself was but an *hors d'oeuvre* to his other accomplishments, one of which was reconstructing a life for himself after the disaster of nine years in a workhouse as a child. Henry II reigned brilliantly, and his son Richard I will mark History to the end of time. Even Henry VIII, who had a deservedly despicable end, made his presence felt by destroying the Catholic church in England, leaving him free to marry and fuck whomever he pleased. The world salutes the originality of the Americans who dare absolutely all, but in the absolute I know of no people who have spawned more original characters than the English, among them Byron and our own Beckford.

In 1797 he ordered the building of an extravaganza with the same original and all-encompassing verve he put in *Vathek*. Called Fonthill Abbey, a manor of crenellated summits that rivaled the Cathedral of Salisbury, massively buttressed at the corners, it had a tower that was 300 feet high, 1/3rd of the Eiffel Tower, just under the height of the Cathedral of Rheims, a tower that fell six times. The Abbey was built by James Wyatt, foremost architect of the period. When the tower came tumbling down later Beckford remarked that ''Wyatt had had an opportunity of raising a splendid monument to his fame, but he missed it.'' The bedrooms were perched 120 feet above the grounds, the pointed-arch windows were wondrously high, and the view of gardens, lakes and the distant rolling hills was simply sublime. As stated, a wall 12 feet high and 8 miles long, topped with iron spikes, surrounded it all. He had harbored the idea of the wall since his visit, at age 17, to Switzerland and his decision at that time to one day build a refuge for animals, as well as a sanctuary for himself from the world's turmoil. Its opening took place in 1800, although far from completed, in the presence of Admiral Lord Nelson, Benjamin Disraeli, and others who dared defy the universal ostracism due to Beckford's reputation of being a boy-lover, a reputation so vile that King George III, who hated homosexuals and not only refused him a peerage, Beckford's life's wish, but was furious that he couldn't have the sodomite put to death.

Fonthill Abbey

Beckford had picked up Franchi in Portugal, as stated, and the man was also responsible for providing Beckford with pornography that Beckford shared with his boys, the nature of which is unknown, but perhaps consisted in part of paintings such as the French king Charles VIII kept with him, purportedly of the most beautiful of his women (he was said to have had two different ones every day, and never slept with the same girl twice).

Army barracks were grounds Franchi scoured for hookups. The soldiers in the barracks at Chelsea in London sold themselves for pocket change and Seven Dials was known as the Holy Land of homosexual cruising, where Franchi was familiar with every darkened niche. On occasion Beckford accompanied him, both in England and abroad. The boys he collected were given nicknames, the Turk, the Ghoul, Monkey, Poupée, Bijou, among many others.

He returned to Portugal where he set up a household that he himself said was more luxurious than that of any European prince: 87 attendants, from French cook to his private doctor, footmen, coachmen, stable boys, and Franchi to supply him with whatever lad struck his eye. He was now, indeed, his own man. Dom Pedro was there, now 20, apparently hounded by women, hungry for his renowned virility. Throughout his travels Beckford collected whatever struck his fancy. His collection was soon world famous, and today every museum and every important private collection has an item that had belonged to him; the National Gallery has 20 of his paintings alone. He bought absolutely everything, an early William Randolph Hearst, and once remarked, "It's cruel to hear of fair boys and dark jade vases and not to buy them."

As for the Abbey, its walls were covered with crimson damask, dark paneling, oak ceilings, and gold wherever possible. It was a cathedral with an over-all impression of Gothic gloom that even Beckford found tomblike. Vaulted rooms fabulous in height, at mind-boggling cost, but the end result was nonetheless an enveloping impression of eerie oppressiveness.

Beckford surrounded himself with boys nearly without number. The two hundred it took to run the Abbey, tend its gardens and stables; even the construction workers were said to number from 300 to 500 at times. He had a fixation for a tightrope walker, part of the Circus Royal, a certain Saunders. Franchi was ordered to contact the lad's father, Abraham Saunders, whose consent Beckford wanted before offering the boy a life-long annuity. Abraham too was given money and his other children gifts. Beckford had inherited £1 million from his father, £121 million in today's money (2015), and when he died at age 84 he still had £80,000 remaining, meaning that he could pay a boy his price. Which brings to mind a story about Lincoln, if the reader would please allow a slight detour. Lincoln, in the presence of his son, was offered a bribe that he refused. The man returned a second time with twice the amount, and Lincoln again refused. When he returned a 3rd time with three times the sum, Lincoln hit him. After the man left, Lincoln's son asked his father to explain himself. "Why did you hit the man during the 3rd visit?" asked the boy. "Because," said Lincoln, "he was getting too near my price." Saunders too may have had his price because one source says he was with Beckford to the end of Beckford's life.

The interior of Fonthill Abbey.

    Beckford's correspondence with Franchi during this period, in Italian, was obsessively centered on Saunders. The translator omitted the dirty parts, and what comes through is glib, faggish discourse that tried, but fails, to be amusing. Saunders is made out to be a celestial object that Beckford promises to shower with gold and take wherever the lad wishes to go (Why not Brazil? he suggests). He urges Franchi to return again and again to Duke Street, Saunder's father's address, to up his offer of money and gifts. Franchi is to convince Abraham that Beckford's only wish is to ''ease the destiny'' of the lad, to offer him a charitable hand. Beckford pleads with Franchi to come to his aide, as only the boy could relieve his distress. ''Nothing else matters,'' he insisted, and it was Franchi's Christian duty, as well as his friendship for Beckford, to go wherever the boy may be and bring him back. Only Franchi, said one letter, had the power to bring renewed life to the miserable carcass that was Beckford, the lovesick lover who drooled for the boy's presence.
    In another letter he begged Franchi to return again to Duke Street to offer his respects and declare his love for the boy's father, mother, brothers, cousins and sisters, and promise them the subsistence that would see them through their remaining years. He warned Franchi to beg in a

chaste fashion, so that he, Beckford, could not be prosecuted for vice. In still another letter he acclaimed the name Duke Street, "Duke of my heart and soul," and again begged Franchi to not be deaf to his pleas.

Beckford finally succeeded in alluring Saunders to a rendezvous in a hotel. He wrote Franchi that the boy was expected to arrive and that he would not be met with kisses as it would be best for Beckford to remain discreet during their first encounter. Beckford even specified that he would talk about any subject under the sun--"about parrots or oranges"--rather than about love. "Decency!" he proclaimed, was the word for the day. He would then retire with his "angel" to the boy's own room which Beckford had prepared for him. He would ask the lad to take pity on him … the final outcome leaving no doubt possible.

His other acquisitions continued unabated. He bought a Turner for £157 when the artist was 25 and the whole of Gibbon's library that he installed in his Abbey, finally finished in 1807. When his debts finally accumulated in dangerous amounts, he was forced to put Fonthill Abbey on the block, which he did in 1822, by way of Christie's. Christie's came out with a catalogue of the Abbey, its interior and furnishings, a catalogue of which 72,000 copies were published that cost a whopping guinea apiece. The Abbey with its tower was so unique that many homes in England were said to have been adorned by a framed copy, taken from the cover of the Christie catalogue. It was purchased by John Farquhar, a gunpowder king who made his fortune by selling his product to troops, especially in India, much of which was used to put down the Great Mutiny of 1857. The price was £330,000 (£26 million today). Like an LOB (leveraged buyout) popular a century and a half later, Farquhar decreased the debt of the purchase by selling off the furnishings and the art Beckford had left behind, a sale so huge that it took place over a period of 37 days. One of the principle buyers was Beckford himself, who bought back part of his own collection at what was a fire sale due to the immense number of items for sale and the depressed market at the time, paying far less than the original price he himself had paid. It didn't help matters when the auction house "salted" the sale with objects that had not belonged to Beckford, putting them among Beckford's collection because Beckford had been known for his great expertise, a guarantee for every object's value. Alas, the Abbey tower collapsed in 1825.

Affable and pleasant, Farquhar was born in England and went to India as a soldier. Badly wounded, he wound up working for a company that produced gunpowder. Obviously highly intelligent and inquisitive, he studied chemistry and came up with a way of making a far better gunpowder than that currently produced. The British put him in charge of his own factory, the basis of his fortune. He increased his knowledge in domains as varied as the classics and mathematics. He sent his money to

London where he soon had half a million pounds (£60 million in 2015 value). On his return to England he walked from the coast to London in order to save coach fare. He arrived so dirty at his bank that his request to see the director was refused until the director was hailed by him when leaving. Even then it took some convincing before the director believed that this was the bank's most fortunate client.

Farquhar continued living in poverty, although it was said he was generous in giving to charities. He bought a brewery and estates, like Beckford's, which he kept until the tower again fell. He died suddenly of a stroke. As he had no immediate family and had left no will, his fortune, £1½ million, went to nephews and nieces.

Fonthill Abbey by Turner.

In addition to his collection of boys and *objets d'art*, he kept a scrapbook of newspaper cuttings that tell us a great deal about the judicial aspects of homosexuality during his lifetime. In 1816, for example, John Eglerton, a married waiter with children was caught *in flagrante delicto* with a stable boy. (There seems to be some highly unscientific rapport between boys and stables, horses and huge horse cocks, which make the lads highly horny.) In this case it took the court ten minutes to sentence Eglerton to death by hanging. Beckford's comment: "I wonder to what deity they're trying to placate with such shocking human sacrifices." At the same time men got off with jail terms for rape and murder, leading Beckford to assert that the risks to an exposed ass must have been far higher.

Beckford went on to buy two residences in Bath, separated by a driveway that he connected with a one-story arch, to which he added two more residences in 1836, all four in Lansdown Crescent.

Lansdown Crescent

He bought the nearby Lansdown Hill where he erected the Lansdown Tower, 154 feet high, known now as the Beckford Tower, today a museum in honor of Beckford.

Beckford Tower

Beckford died at Lansdown Crescent in 1844, supposedly in excellent health up to the end. "When I am summoned I must go," he had said, "though I would not much mind living another hundred years, and, as far as my health goes at present, I see no reason why I should not." He was accompanied by his daughter to whom he had written a telegram: "Come quick." He was laid in a sarcophagus of pink granite which he had designed himself, placed on a mound as had been the custom of Saxon kings, from whom he claimed to be descended, as peerage, as said, had been a life-long obsession. Later his daughter would have him reinterred near the Lansdown Tower, the construction of which he had painstakingly supervised, a phallic symbol that in itself summed up his life.

BYRON

1788 – 1824

Byron lived in an age when men were hanged for their love of males and/or pilloried, caged in public and punched by sticks, eyes stove in and throats pierced, at times causing death. The high and mighty in England didn't necessarily escape (although most did), as shown by Oscar Wilde's trial for homosexuality, a man whose plays were immensely popular then as they are today. There was also the threat of blackmail that led to many suicides. To be hanged, both penetration and ejaculation had to be proved in a court of law, no easy affair. In France laws against sodomy were dropped after the Revolution, in 1791, and many other countries like Italy and Spain followed. But not England. Yet school was a protected sanctum, where boys could enjoy their puberty more or less unhampered. Boys were locked in their dormitories at night, left to themselves, at times exhausting their young bodies in orgies that would have impressed the Romans. *All* boarding schools were rife with sex. H. Montgomery Hyde, who later lost his seat in the House of Commons because of his plea for understanding concerning homosexuals, quoted a student, Addington Symonds: ''The talk in the dormitories and studies was of the grossest character, with repulsive scenes of onanism, mutual masturbation and obscene orgies of naked boys in bed together. There was no refinement, just animal lust.'' The first order that Thackeray received on his first day at school from a schoolmate was ''Come & frig me,'' he wrote later. Byron had innumerable lovers, and it is believed that his sex life began as early as age 9 when a servant aroused him sexually by taking him in her mouth. It had long been a custom in Sardinia for mothers to soothe their baby boys by taking the entirety of their sexual apparatus in their mouths, a measure said to have instantly calmed theirs sons. Later Byron claimed to have read Arabian erotica at age 10. His earliest pre-school crushes seemed to have been with girls, and girls would bring him pleasure throughout his life (pleasure for Byron's friends too, as Byron would often turn his mistresses over to them). Had not the dangers of the pillory, hanging, blackmail and public scandal been real, he might have had far more homosexual experiences than heterosexual.

In 1808 he decided to go to the Orient. Boys he met along the way stirred him sexually and even in Falmouth he wrote to friends at Cambridge about the remarkably handsome lads, one of which he compared to Apollo's lover Hyacinth (1). He employed the word coitus throughout his letters, perhaps taking it from the *Satyricon* where Eumolpus tells how, after much trickery, he had full and complete intercourse with the boy he had been after (*plenum et optabilem coitum*). He went to Albania where he found the most splendid boys he had ever seen, and then went on to Athens where he heard the story of Hadrian and Antinous (2), and where he went from boy to boy, writing home that he had

had 200 couplings ("two hundred *pl and opt Cs*"), so many that he was becoming tired of them, he wrote. In Athens he visited the site of the two lovers Aristogeiton and Harmodius. He went on to Leuctra where the Sacred Band of lovers defeated the Spartans and then to the Thermopylae where Leonidas saved us all from Persian barbarism at the head of 150 Spartan couples formed of lovers and their belovèds. He swam in the Hellespont and went on to Troy, battlegrounds of Achilles and Patroclus (2). In a letter, he regretted that the shepherds in his day did not resemble, in beauty, Paris, the abductor of Helen.

He had to be careful in what he wrote home: In one letter he admitted to receiving "as many kisses as would have sufficed for a boarding school." In another "one boy had ambrosial curls hanging down his amiable back" and in another place he and a boy "traveled very much enamoured." In still another letter he asks the reader to tell a friend that he had finally "had" a Greek boy they had known at Cambridge, whom Byron looked up in his native Athens, one of the few he didn't pay for.

He returned to England where men were being hung for "unnatural crimes," two per year. Prison and blackmail, as well as being ostracism by one's peers, were current. The accusation of having committed a homosexual crime would bring out a mob of hundreds into the streets, and the accused had to be protected by large numbers of police. A lieutenant was caught amusing himself with a drummer boy of 16, two years after Byron's return; both were hanged (see chapter on The White Swan Scandal). In the crowd observing the hanging was the Duke of Cumberland, who just missed inheriting the English throne. Nine months before the hanging his valet had been found dead, killed by the duke, thought some, because the valet was blackmailing him for having sex with another of the duke's male servants--every reason for Byron to make good use of whatever heterosexual blood he had within him when seeking pleasure. That he did not exclusively do so is proof of his deep attraction to boys.

When a friend of Byron's drowned at Cambridge, Byron, perhaps inspired by the early death, made out a will in which he left £7,000, $300,000 in today's money, to Nicolo Giraud in Athens. Nicolo had been the Greek boy from Cambridge Byron had finally seduced. Nicolo seems to have been a boy of quality, but this was not necessary always the case for Byron, who seems to have had a weakness for effeminate lads, an English paradox because many Englishmen can be supremely masculine, as were the soldiers in the barracks at Chelsea in London who sold themselves for pocket money. As Byron also liked girls, he may have been more active in sex with boys than passive, and nearly any buttocks would fill the bill, especially in hot sexually charged regions like Albania, Greece and Turkey. On the other hand, the only certainty in sexuality is that nothing is certain.

After losing the Cambridge friend by drowning, he lost another boy, whom he claimed had been the greatest love of his very young years, John Edlestone, to tuberculosis. He wrote poems to the boy but so great was homosexual punishment that one understands nearly nothing of their tender relationship from Byron's writings.

With the publication of *Childe Harold* Byron would become a world-renowned poet, and would attract a succession of women mistresses, from Caroline Lamb, who would torture him with her public scandals, tantrums and spying, to the Countess of Oxford, and then his own half-sister Augusta Leigh, the most perverse and perhaps the deepest of his female attachments. He then took up with Annabella Milbanke who knew about his homosexuality and perhaps thought she could save him. He apparently did too because they married.

As feared, Caroline Lamb decided to avenge herself, at first accusing Byron of being a homosexual, then of committing incest. Annabella, it seems, spent her time trying to keep him from killing himself. Incest was illegal, but the penalty was far less severe than for homosexuality; that Byron had entered into an incestuous relationship, so venerated by the pharaohs, so heinous for us, was proof that for this boy there were really no earthly limits, and worse would come when he tried to penetrate the 11-year-old daughter of his mistress.

He went to Geneva where it is said he was shunned, while in London a newspaper, the *Champion,* related that Byron was involved in a scandal but placed itself above printing the exact nature. There followed around seven years of largely heterosexual activity, including four years in Italy with a certain countess. He had met her at age 31, she 20, and her husband 54, who appealed to the pope when she left him, but because of Byron's celebrity the pope refused to intervene. Byron was happy with what the publicity was doing for his reputation as a heterosexual in Britain, but as Molière had so rightly written, *Tout le plaisir de l'amour est dans le changement.* Byron therefore decided to return to Greece, and to boys.

There he met the Chalandrutsanos family, consisting of a mother who had fallen on bad times, her three daughters and Lukas, her 15-year-old son who was busy fighting the Turks for Greek independence. Youth from all over Europe, Germany, France, Spain and Italy were flocking to Greece to help the Greeks win their freedom, but due to Greek incompetence, whose who survived returned in rags. Byron took Lukas in hand and wherever they went Byron was well received, thanks to his reputation and wealth. He provided the boy with a uniform and pistols, and welcomed him into his entourage as a page, the usual cover for rent boys. He had Lukas read ancient Greek texts, certainly those tainted with Greek love, and like any boy Lukas' age, and having lived under the Turks, the boy certainly recognized the intentions behind Byron's largesse.

Even at age 23 Byron had envisioned suicide, but at that age he was sexually fulfilled, and so such thoughts meant little in comparison to now, nearly 36, his hair thinning, his teeth bad and his body fat. He was far from sexually satiated now, so thoughts of suicide, on the battlefield, alongside his Lukas, were attractive. The revenge of age is total. Byron's reputation and money could buy him consolation, but the mirror was there to remind him of the inevitable ravages of time. Lucky were those like Achilles, like Patroclus, Alexander and Hephaestion, who left early, in possession of their physical force and beauty.

Lukas was perhaps there to consol him because he shared Byron's bed, as related by numerous sources. But Lukas appeared unhappy, and Byron's gifts to him, gilded pistols, gold-laced jackets and a beautiful saddle, seemed to have done little to lessen what appeared to have been the boy's disdain for Byron. Perhaps the boy in no way shared Byron's bent, perhaps he would have preferred someone younger with a more beautiful body. A man throwing himself at a disdainful boy is sad, especially for a boy who had known the luxury of love and fulfilled desire since his early puberty, as had Byron.

Byron wrote poems to the boy, so sexually discreet that it's difficult to know what he's talking about, yet in the reality of his daily life he was telling friends that his "cock still has spring in it".

This may have been so, but there was daily less spring in his health. He suffered from fevers, perhaps the malaria he had contracted in the South of France as a boy, and syphilis. He had dizzy spells and weakness. Bloodletting, still popular, in no way helped, and some say it even killed him. In 1824 he was carried away by fever, certainly not to a better place since it's difficult to imagine a destiny as fulfilling in love, in art, in sexual bliss as that having been lived by Byron. He died at 36, the exact age of his father. A few months later, victim of the Greek War for Independence, Lukas followed.

When I began this chapter I imagined Byron a physically beautiful hero who has won the admiration of generations through his poetry. In reality he had himself painted when he was in flower, rare moments between bouts of obesity. His rage knew no limits when he suffered the pain of his clubfoot and found out that the reason was his mother's corsets, trying to limit her own spread, uncaring of the physical damage to her son, as he too would be uncaring of how he damaged others. The world owed him a never-ending debt for his handicap, placing him above laws and rules, allowing him to force himself on children and to bed his sister; his money permitted every excess, his position every depravity. And in the end he found himself slavering at the feet of a boy, one that not even the gifts of silver pistols, gold-threaded jackets and fine leather saddles could entice to favor the foul-breathed, fat baron, at his feet.

The Byron family history is one of licentiousness and handsome men, both of which very often go in tandem. Byron's father, called Mad Jack, passed his time in Paris gambling and going through a limitless number of females. Only when in bottomless debt, at age 22--having been cut off for years from his family as its black sheep--did he meet and mate with the Marchioness of Carmarthen who craved him for his beauty and virility, and who left her husband, taking with her £4,000 of yearly income, a fortune. They married and produced Augusta, Byron's half-sister, who would, in the tradition of Caligula, become one of Bryon's many mistresses. The Marchioness died, perhaps under the hands of her husband, although Byron declared his father innocent of any wrongdoing, and as for his licentiousness, was it his father's fault that women threw themselves at him? One of these women was Byron's mother, Catherine Gordon, plump but possessing £30,000 and her own castle. Her family was described as having been bloodthirsty killers, generation after generation, but this only concerned the men. As for the Byrons, his first important ancestor was John Byron who bought his manor from Henry VIII. Another Byron had been shipwrecked off Patagonia. Still another was known as the Wicked Lord who set up his own whorehouse where one night he plunged his sword into the stomach of Viscount Chaworth in an upper floor of the brothel. This Byron had nine children, one of which had been our Byron's dad, Mad Jack.

Mad Jack bled his wife, Byron's mother, white, forcing her to sell her castle, farm lands and woods to pay for his need to assuage, in luxury, his gambling and his balls--not put too fine a point on it. Catherine's pain did not end in the long and painful birth of Byron. The boy was born clubfooted, a handicap that would handicap his mind and personality from his first breath, an impediment that would cause him anguish until his death, at first physical pain during his infancy, mental hardship afterwards. He never forgave his mother whom he accused of injuring him for life due to her insistence on wearing the tightest corsets. Rich, she could have had whomever she wished; now she was weighed down by a husband who wouldn't touch her, a step-daughter, Augusta, she immediately farmed out to whichever of her relatives would take her in, turning the poor girl into a timid, emotional recluse. Catherine was weighed down too by a son who despised her with each painful step he took (later, when his own beauty was in decline, he would realize that she was the only person who was truly selfless and had truly loved him). He called himself the *diable boiteux,* the lame devil, and felt life owned him a debt, its permission for him to commit every excess.

Every excess was what his father was at that moment committing. He returned to London but lived down the street from his wife, requesting money before begging for it, before abandoning son and wife to return to

France where he lived with his sister, Francis, as dissolute as he. She made love to whoever was available, as did her brother Mad Jack, both comparing the sexual endurance and the quirks of their respective lovers, until they themselves fell into Caligulan incest, which they eventually enlarged to all comers.

With the death of their mother, and the hope of a heritage, his sister Francis returned to London. She set herself up there and he tried to entice her back by writing about his loves, in hopes of making her jealous. In reality, he had more women than even he could satisfy. About one woman he wrote to his sister, ''She told me I did it so well she spent twice.'' About another, ''She is the best piece I ever fucked.''

In the meantime Byron's mother was teaching him something about feminine inconsistency by showering him with love and the best in clothes money could buy, but during angry spells she called him a damn lame brat and assured him he was just like his worthless father. It's unsurprising that Byron was soon known for his own unbridled rages.

In France Jack was assailed by creditors who took his every possession to pay his debts. He had also been coughing up blood. Perhaps luckily for everyone concerned, including Jack, he died at age 36, the same age as Byron who inherited all his vices, down to incest, all except Mad Jack's gambling. Jack had been a man who had lived the lives of a dozen men, just as his son would, who would die while still in beauty, biting lustily into life until his last breath.

Catherine's maid put little Bryon on the path of his father at age 9, in 1799. In her bed she masturbated him while doing herself, then gave herself freely to coachmen, while beating the boy mercilessly when she felt like it. He later wrote that his sexual awakening had come so early that no one would believe it, but was sorrowful because it was combined with the beatings and the inconsistency of the maid who abandoned him for other lovers.

Mad Jack nonetheless left his son his heritage: One day he would become the fifth Lord of Byron.

He entered Harrow at age 12 and it was paradise. The headmaster, Dr. Joseph Drury, immediately recognized the boy's terrible self-consciousness due to his leg in irons, but like everyone who would meet him, he fell in love with his charm and beauty. From then on Byron would use his leg as an arm to initiate sympathy and protection, his charm and beauty would do the rest. Although not at first. At first the heathen brutality of boys made him the target of the cruelest allusions to his deformity.

It was during summer vacation from Harrow that he first met his half-sister Augusta, 17, she with whom he would repeat his father's incest.

Back at Harrow after the summer holidays, Byron became popular by helping new first year students, some of whom became dedicated to him in thanks. He would write, "My school friendships were *with me passions*," his italics. One of his passions was 11-year-old John Fitzgibbon, Earl of Clare, about whom he wrote, 18 years later, "I never hear the word *'Clare'* without a beating of the heart--even now." He left Harrow at the age of 16, immortalized by Straton:

>A hairless boy of twelve is sublime,
>A youth thirteen is in his prime.
>Fourteen is a sweeter flower still,
>While fifteen a man's heart will fill.
>Sixteen is destined for the gods divine,
>Seventeen is for Zeus' bed, not mine.

He entered Cambridge at the age of 17, now prey to Zeus, predator to the rest. As a noble he was allowed to wear extravagant garb, a robe bordered with gold embroidery. "I was superb," he writes. Juan Borgia, too, dressed sumptuously during the Renaissance: "As virile as his father, slim waisted and certain of his sex appeal, Juan swaggered through the streets of Rome in what can only be described as gorgeous attire, a cloak of gold brocade, jewel-encrusted waistcoats and silk shirts, skin-tight trousers with drop fronts--cloth attached by ribbons that would free a man's loins when he wished to piss. This beautiful, gorgeously clad body, with 30 golden ducats still in his belt purse, was fished up from the Tiber, to the grief-stricken horror of his father who locked himself away from public view for three days." (An extract from my book *Cesare Borgia, His Violent Life, His Violent Times*.) This is the reason I'm personally so in love with the Renaissance; the reason I spurn post-Shakespeare English foppish dandies. He wrote that his time was "filled with dissipation, with eating, drinking and sleeping, his table stacked with invitations," his bed certainly warmed by bedfellows. To my mind this brings the image of lads tidily arranging their clothes while talking about the robes they would wear later for supper, or making spiritual puns on this or that of their recent lovers, then making love of their own, like taking sherry, devoid of the slightest virility, nothing of Juan Borgia. Where there is no hunger there is no lust, and Byron was satiated all of his life.

Cambridge was of little educational value. Yet he had picked up his knowledge somewhere, most probably at Harrow and with private tutors before entering Harrow, as his mother was set on him having the best in every domain. The more she denied her husband, the more she gave to her boy. Byron was reading at age 3, and his years in Cambridge were certainly not entirely worthless, although intellectually shallow. A European education is opposite to that in America where, except for those having rich and enlightened parents who prepare boys for entry into Princeton, Harvard and Yale, thanks to private institutions, education on the high-school level for less fortunate boys is often woefully empty. Whereas American universities are true monuments to learning. In Europe the *lycées* are sites of intense instruction, and those who make it into the top schools afterwards sail through with nothing of the workload known to their American counterparts.

He went to brothels, the price being venereal disease that the doctors treated with leeches to bring down the swelling. One of his lovers was a choir boy of 15, John Edleston, for whom Byron, 17, was a man of the world. (It appears that for university students choir boys were redolent of dancehall girls for adults; it was good form for each boy to have sexual access to at least one.) ''I *love* him more than any human being,'' he wrote to a friend. It would be a deep and long-lasting love for Edleston.

As I wrote, an education at Cambridge at that period was notoriously lamentable. Getting in was everything, because afterwards nothing was demanded. There were few lessons and few hours of study. Everything was based on money, money that paid for his clothes, his meals, his servant, the women who made him ill and the doctors that cured him with middle-ages efficiency. His money and title perhaps played a part in his seduction of Edleston. Certainly not his phsique. At age 18 he weighed over 200 pounds for a height of 5' 8''. He wasn't chubby, he was fat, an inheritance from his mother who was fat all her life, having attracted Byron's father by her castle and fortune, and even then she was open and accepting of any man who would deign accept her largesse for a little bodily warmth.

He wrote to his Harrow love Claire and they exchanged letters on the cures they were taking for venereal diseases, Claire, as mentioned, treated with leeches, Byron with a powder, most probably mercury for syphilis. The illness went on for several months, which nonetheless ended (or went into remission) with his losing a great deal of weight, a temporary benefit for a boy who would be remembered as a poetic Don Juan. Between bouts of venereal disease, which made him often ill, he would literally fuck his brains out with whatever came to hand. It seems that the end of the fever always brought on a period of intense sexual activity, acting as a kind of aphrodisiac. At that moment it was prostitutes he turned to. There was one who was, it would seem, sexually insatiable and thusly pleased Byron greatly. She ended up carrying a baby that Byron paid to have aborted. Sadly Edleston, who appears to have been a sincere lad, sincerely in love with Byron, was replaced by this whore, in the tradition of Byron's father and grandfather and all the other horny rakes that preceded him.

After the whore came the gifted son of a butcher, John Cowell, whom he helped to enter Eton. The boy's parents, flattered by Byron's nobility, allowed their 15-year-old boy to spend long weekends with Byron. Cowell did so well in school that he won a scholarship to university. Later he wrote Byron to express his gratitude. From his letter it is obvious that Byron was and would rest the most important influence in the boy's life.

At age 21 Byron took his seat in the House of Lords. A new lord who took on a new page and lover, Robert Rushton, 17, but flew into a rage when his valet, William Fletcher, took the boy to a whorehouse for his very first prostitute.

It's easy to imagine these young boys, a lad who sings in a choir, another saved from cutting up pigs by the intervention of a veritable lord, falling under the sway of this tubby boy who had began his apprenticeship of life so young that he had by now personally known every minor earthly corruption, stunning in his lace, bowed to by his valet, offering fine dinners among spiritual friends, all of whom possessed to a perfection that special way of speaking known to the nobility, those like Byron whose only thought was to fill their stomachs and empty their scrotums.

He left London for Greece with some pals under terrible auspices, having had a fight with his mother over money, as that was her interest to Byron as it had been to his father. She had apparently told him his mind was as twisted as his body.

He went to Falmouth, as recounted in the Forward and saw boys of such beauty that he was hoping he would have, during his travels, intercourse to his heart's content (*coitum plenum & optabilem*, the words he used in a letter to a friend).

They went to Albania, ruled by the Turks. Their first major stop was the city of Jannina. He was housed in the mansion of a Greek merchant and met the local scholar, a Greek with whom he spoke in Latin. The Greek told him that homosexuality was openly practiced and that in the absence of girls boys had only themselves or masturbation for pleasure. The vizier and his sons welcomed Byron. The vizier, Ali Pasha, offered Byron an Albanian soldier named Vassily as his guide. Vassily had recently killed a 17-year-old girl and her sixteen companions when Ali Pasha's daughter-in-law claimed that the girl had led her husband astray. All 17 were sewn in sacks and thrown from the top of Ali Pasha's castle into the sea below. Later Vassali was given to Byron as a present. In return Byron offered Ali Pasha a superb rifle. He regretfully left Albania, with Vassily and some guards provided by Ali Pasha, sad to leave a land of beautiful men devoted to boy-love, as pagan as Eden before the Fall.

In Greece he met and loved Eustatius Georgiou, a beauty who sold himself to the highest bidder. Byron moved on to Delphi: ''Delphi. In the beginning the gods freed two high-flying eagles, one from the East, the other from the West. They met on the lofty crags of a great mountain that loomed over a jagged valley and the far-off port of Cirrha. Here was the sacred center of the universe; here was the spiritual navel of the Hellens; here was Delphi, home of Apollo.

"For Apollo had left his birthplace on Cycladic Delos to teach Man wisdom by revealing to him the future. Apollo traveled to the heights of Mount Parnassus where he destroyed the snake-like dragon, Python, its guardian. Then, with the help of the Muses and the consent of Mother Earth, he recruited sailors from a passing Cretan ship whom he made priests, and irreproachable villagers from the nearby village of Krissa whom he ordained priestesses, sometimes called Pythonesses in memory of the dragon. He built a temple, initiated the love of the arts, taught moderation and humaneness in all things, and himself tried to exemplify the virtuous life.

"Now Delphi, wind-swept haven in the bosom of Mount Parnassus, snow-bound home of the Muses, misty abode of oracular Apollo, open your gates to" the English boy Byron who has come as a suppliant to learn his fate. (An extract from my book *TROY*, the end of which I've slightly altered.)

There were no hotels in Athens at the time but there were tourists, which made Byron's arrival far less noted than in tourist-free Albania. They were offered rooms by the British consul. They visited archeological sites, guided by Giovanni Lusieri, responsible for depriving the Parthenon of its façade, the Elgin Marbles now in the British Museum.

He and his friends visited bordellos, one of the friends noting the number of climaxes he achieved. They visited other sites noted in the Forward. Byron had already met Lusieri's brother-in-law Nicolo Giraud who became Byron's favorite and whom Byron seemed to have taught as much as he could of the arts of sexual pleasure, as Nicolo was very young. But the boy wouldn't give himself as completely as Byron wished, as Byron complained that there was as yet no *pl & opt C* (complete and fulfilling intercourse). He nonetheless wrote that he personally was an attraction to boys, and that he had found himself in a boy heaven--for a price, naturally.

He came down with a fever so terrible it was feared he would die, but afterwards he noted something that would prove always true for him, as already noted, an enormous regain in sexual ardor which pushed him to enter into **200** *pl & opt C*.

Byron

Childe Harold was published at a time when even Boccaccio was considered as obscene. It was at first rejected. At that same moment he learned of his mother's death. He had to borrow the money to return home where his grief, certainly sincere, was overwhelming. He realized that he had lost, at age 46 (from undisclosed causes) the only person who had ever loved him for himself. He was now truly alone, and although he would be encumbered by a plethora of willing bodies to come, alone he would remain until the end of his life. He learned, too, of the suicides of two of his dearest friends, proof that wealth, beauty and nobility were far from being life's panacea. He made out his own will, leaving £7,000 to Nicolo Giraud "on his attaining the age of twenty-one". His page Robert Rushton would receive £1,000 when he to came of age. His relationship with Robert was the only homosexual friendship he would ever admit to.

Byron at his most beautiful.

It was now that he met Caroline Lamb, married to an older husband, William Lamb, whom she had genuinely loved, but now wanted Byron more. Their sexual relationship was heated for both, but eventually petered out, perhaps due in part to the scandals Caroline wrought wherever she went. Byron went to see William Lamb's mother for advice, Lady Melbourne, known as the Spider, a spider in every domain of social congress, especially sexual. The 62-year-old woman was highly flattered by Byron's attentions, attentions which would soon have him probing her inners with his dick. She decided that the best way out of his problems with Caroline would be for Bryon to marry. Byron agreed, as long as the future wife was wealthy enough to care for his needs, exactly the reason his father had had for marrying Byron's mother. She found him Annabella Milbanke, the daughter of her brother Sir Ralph Milbanke, and her financial prospects were glorious. Caroline tried to get Byron back, even showing up at his residence disguised as a boy. That didn't seem to work as she was shown away before anything physical had had time to take place. Revealingly, it was at that time that Byron wrote to a friend stating that he had once loved both swimming and making love, but that now he swam only when he fell into the water and "I don't make love until almost obliged." He also made an interesting observation: he hated watching a woman eat, but loved watching a boy do so. His life seemed unenviable because now he had to juggle his relationship with three women, old Lady Melbourne, rich Annabella Milbanke, and Caroline in order to keep her from more scandalous behavior, although he may still have cared for her sexually, especially as she was still young and eminently boyish. If this were not enough, he then took as mistress Lady Oxford, age 40, who had many lovers as well as a husband, but Byron seemed to find this natural as she had little time for seduction left to her.

The height of horrors came when Lady Oxford found him trying to force an entry into her 11-year-old daughter. He was sent away but sustained the inconvenience thanks to the good news that his book was a sell-out. The orientalism of the locations in the poems did wonders as did his bad-boy reputation (although none of his admirers knew about the backroom scenes of sex with boys, with children and incest). To help things along, Byron had himself painted in Albanian dress.

Byron in Albanian splendor.

Caroline capped this all off by stabbing herself with scissors in public, careful to do minimal damage. The whole pathetic mess, fake suicides, effeminate Greeks lovers, sex with matrons, with children, with hysterical mistresses, with his sister, with choir boys, was so lamentable that one finishes by pitying the now largely unread poet.

He made his sister pregnant. She would eventually give him a girl he was surprised to find physically normal as children of incest were supposed to have been born deformed (and he didn't seem to have cared, one way or the other). They both traveled to London and then to the family manor, bought by his ancestor from Henry VIII, the very foundation of his nobility, with the aim of selling it. It was the first time Augusta had seen the Abbey. The manor was magnificent and his digs in London were sumptuous. The sitting room soared two storeys in height, with arched windows giving onto a garden.

Newstead Abbey, Byron's manor.

His presence was required at the marriage of the Earl of Portsmouth. Portsmouth was said to have been insane but wasn't committed to an asylum because of his nobility. He was tricked into the marriage, arriving in dirty clothes that the girl's father--a lawyer who oversaw Portsmouth's estate and was aware, therefore, of his wealth and his inclination to beating all around him, from servants to animal--exchanged for formal marriage attire. Byron walked the girl down the isle; she supposedly giggled as he reminded her that as a schoolboy he had been the first to fuck her. Years later the marriage was annulled; the girl had by then three children, one named Byron; and then she vanished from the face of the earth, never to be seen again.

Byron, in tandem with his sister, chose Annabella Milbanke for wife, once assured of a stupendous dowry of £20,000 and a heritage that would assure many thousand more. Had he managed to sell his manor he most likely would not have married, but the marriage came off, although he dreaded it and Annabella, perhaps sensing that something was wrong, had offered to give him his freedom before exchanging vows. She was deliriously happy and he, by necessity, fucked her that night on the couch, before dinner, bloodied because she had been a virgin. He then told here they would have separate bedrooms as he never slept in the same bed with his women. Byron would later have his memoirs destroyed, but the man who did so wrote that that night Byron had awoken and had cried out, God I am in Hell! Even more unbelievably, Annabella had convinced herself that her only true friend in the world was Augusta, to whom she confided the despair of her marriage. Augusta immediately relayed every word to Byron. Annabella finished by accepting whatever scraps he left her. He continued to fuck Augusta and only turned to his wife when Augusta wasn't available.

No matter how much Annabella brought in, Byron spent more, and eventually a bailiff came to seize the furniture. Byron kept on running up debts and began to drink heavily. When he learned that Annabella was pregnant, he became wild, smashing what furniture was left, firing his pistol within his home, and shouted that he hoped both Annabella and the child in her womb would both perish. Augusta was now in control of the household, trying to bring sincere succor to both Annabella and Byron. Days before the birth of his and Annabella's child he forced her to have sex with him, but when this continued right up to the delivery, she refused and he ended up raping her. From that moment on her maid kept her rooms locked, and physically barred the entrance to Byron. It is actually believed that he tried to kill the unborn child by frightening Annabella to death. Four weeks after the baby's birth he ordered both out of the house. She left and Byron would never see either again.

He continued drinking, he became ill, he had memory loses, weeping jags, bouts of depression and violence. The problem for Byron was how to keep his sanity. The problem for Annabella was how to keep her child, for in Victorian England the husband had total and absolute rights to it. He could have taken it whenever he wished, and given the nature of the animal, he could have taken its virginity at any time too. The only way out for Annabella was to construct a case so damning against him that the courts would deprive him of his rights to the little girl. Annabella--and here there is no doubt possible--had truly loved the man. But from now on he ceased to exist as a human being in her eyes. Yet she held her head high. She was only a woman against him and against nearly every man in society who realized that if she won they would be open to any form of female aggression. Their survival as the ruling class was Byron's survival. How pitiful it was that later, in Greece, he would be unable to hold his own head high, as high as she could now, when brought low by a lad of 15, groveling at the feet of a lad of 15, begging for a few moments of shared warmth with a lad of 15.

Caroline Lamb then weighed in in favor of Annabella, informing the world that Byron was homosexual (Byron had told her about his relations with Robert Rushton). Byron immediately realized that a divorce would be long and drawn out and *public*, that his homosexuality would be revealed in the newspapers and perhaps even his incest (and what if Lady Oxford came forward with his attempted rape of her 11-year-old daughter?). Only a legal separation was therefore possible, one that Annabella would agree to only if she could retain her child. Augusta was amazingly evenhanded, and its clear that she truly felt for Annabella, while hoping to do nothing that would harm her brother and lover. She knew about Byron's homosexuality and she knew too that if even a whiff of it hit the public he would be utterly destroyed. Then Annabella released a bomb. She told Byron's lawyers that she knew about his incest with Augusta. In reality she couldn't *not* have known, because they were doing it downstairs while she was upstairs in her rooms; indeed, she had heard everything for months. (The flooring was so thin that when Byron was working downstairs he would ask Annabella to stop walking about, as it disturbed his concentration.)

Byron still hesitated because he was hoping to milk Annabella for as much money as he could suck from the marrow of her bones (no exaggeration, as Augusta was shocked, during a visit to Annabella, to find her reduced to skin and bones by her effort to save her child). Then Annabella dropped the *atomic* bomb: Byron had raped her during the final days of her pregnancy, attested to by her maid and his valet (who were man and wife--the husband being Robert Rushton), by *sodomizing* her, the absolute in scandals.

Byron signed the civil separation, locked up his rooms, and fled to Europe.

He went to Switzerland where he took the best lodgings and met Shelley. Shelley is known to have written the best description of orgasm ever, according to some, a perfect example of Victorian clarity:

> The Serchio, twisting forth
> Between the marble barriers which it clove
> At Ripafratta, leads through the dread chasm
> The wave that died the death which lovers love,
> Living in what it sought; as if this spasm
> Had not yet passed, the toppling mountains cling,
> But the clear stream in full enthusiasm
> Pours itself on the plain.

Byron and Shelley got on well as both had shared a similar background and had gone to the best schools, but Byron was a successful poet, while Shelley had written little, and what he wrote had been ridiculed.

Shelley was a man of my heart, the true hero of his chapter. His sexuality, as far as men went, is unknown as his wife Mary was said to have destroyed anything compromising. But we know that at school he was genuinely despised by his comrades because he refused to enter into their senseless activities. He was thrown out of Oxford due to his atheism, having written *The Necessity of Atheism,* as well as his anti-monarchism, found in his *Poetical Essay on the Existing State of Things*. (Two stands dear to my heart, as well as the ban on mutilating boys through circumcision.) He had a keen interest in science, which led to his blowing up a tree on the Oxford campus and his electrifying the bronze handle of the door leading to his rooms, to the intense surprise of his visitors. Atheism and anti-monarchism are of interest only so far as one is unable to understand why men, in our scientific and democratic day and age, continue to fall back on the voodoo-like crutch of religion, and why one allows oneself to accept second-rate citizenship under holier-than-thou nobles. What does count are intellectual strides forward, and in this Shelley was infinitely more important than Byron who publicly, wretchedly, proclaimed his belief in a higher being just to gain access to Annabella Milbanke's fortune. And, cherry on the cake,

Shelley didn't rape children or have incest with his four sisters or go crawling at the heels of a 15-year-old boy. And when he died he was lithe and beautiful, not a slob so fat the knuckles of his hands looked as if they would burst.

Shelley

He eloped at age 19 with Harriet, age 16, but the marriage didn't work out and Shelley began to learn Italian, seemingly certain of two things, that his future was in Italy and that he hadn't long to live. Shelley had a friend who ran a bookshop, William Godwin. Godwin had three daughters, two adopted and one from his wife and his wife's lover. They were Fanny, Claire and Mary. All three loved Shelley and Shelly had sexual congress with Mary and Claire, but it was Mary he loved and threatened suicide if she wouldn't eventually wed him. Fanny, left out, killed herself. Harriet, after having two children by Shelley, fell in love with a Lt. Colonel who went off on maneuvers. Harriet's family, who disapproved of her lover, had Harriet's landlady destroy letters from the Lt. Colonel. Believing she had been abandoned, she drowned herself, although carrying her lover's child. His wife dead, Shelley could now wed Mary.

In the interim Claire, having been rejected by Shelley, threw herself on Byron, literally begging him to have intercourse at an inn near his residence. As she was 17, he surrendered. Claire bore him a girl. Byron had gone off to Venice and Shelley, Mary and Claire decided to visit him so he could meet his child. Both men got on beautifully, but alas two of Shelley's children, a boy and a girl, died of fevers. Shelley then had a child, perhaps Claire's, but this baby too soon died. Mary had two more children, a boy and a girl.

Byron went on to Milan and Rome where his presence brought out society girls who shivered before his reputation, but he preferred the far less complexity of male friendships. In Verona he chipped some pieces from Juliette's tomb as a souvenir, not forgetting that Shakespeare's heroin had died at age 13. In Venice he had gorgeous digs, his own horses and had hired his own gondola. Unlimited mistresses followed, but sex with women had always plagued his life with complications and this would continue: outraged husbands and jealousy among the women to the point of their attacking each other in front of Byron for his favors, often in public. There were balls, with women he took in every possible niche and hideaway, in every possible position. His potency was revived and he became as insatiable as his women. He took rich mistresses, at times for months, but they knew that to keep him they would have to cut him considerable slack, which they did. In letters to male friends he even joked at the dimensions of their clitorises. One left her brother, from whom she'd had a child, for him.

He received word that his manor had finally been sold, for nearly £100,000, millions in today's money, enough to see him through many years of future pleasure. And pleasure there was. In a letter to a friend he wrote of a beauty he loved to ''push *in*,'' whom he ''fucked twice a day for the last six weeks.'' He had a child, a girl, by one of them, and wrote to a friend, ''My bastard came three days ago.''

From here on he began reverting back to homosexual sex. Someone who met him at the time stated that although he was around 30 he looked at least 40, his face was bloated, he was fat, ''the knuckles of his hands were lost in fat,'' and his hairline was receding.

He returned to Venice where he took up his friendship with Shelley. Out sailing, Shelley was caught up in a sudden storm and drowned, along with two friends. Byron went looking for him and it was at sea that Byron and others found Shelley's remains, barely enough to have cremated. He was 29.

The cremation of Shelley/Byron looking on

Byron sincerely mourned him as the finest, most unselfish man he had ever known. Mary went on to write *Frankenstein*.

Byron traveled on the Greece where he took up residence in various locals, hiring pages that the Greeks knew to be synonyms to rent boys. The last one was Lukas Chalandrutsanos, age 15, before whom he groveled until fever carried him away.

Byron's outlandish reputation is based on his being a dissolute and ever-randy bisexual master of orgies, on his staged portraits in which he is the personification of male splendor, and his publications, that I must leave entirely to the reader's judgment, judgment based on their appearance in other books than this, as I personally prefer clarity to Victorian obscurantism. Like the very young and the very old, he lived outside the circle of life. He made his own laws and rules; life owed him every favor to compensate for his infirmity; and the planets had obligingly aligned to give birth to this, their most unique creation. I have no idea if he succeeded his life, but I know that he succeeded his afterlife, because he will remain in our imaginations until the end of time. At age 36 he left the stage a little late, as he had not escaped the mutilation and humiliation of old age. He had known horrendous ups-and-downs, a rollercoaster that is the very definition of life. He was certainly far too in love with himself to wish others happiness, so it is I who wish the reader bountiful *pl and opt Cs*.

VICTORIAN TIMES

VICTORIAN RENT BOYS

    In Victorian times a man's sexuality seems to me to have been the strangest that ever existed in our society. On the one hand most men seemed to have put women on pedestals and succeeded in controlling their urges, while on the other hand there were never so many male brothels. The sending of telegrams exploded when it was found out that men could hire the boys who delivered them for a few kopeks, a boon for the men, and badly needed additional income for the boys. After all, what a healthy lad did by himself in the privacy of his own room could just as easily be turned into profit, especially as the assignations lasted literally just minutes. Men were often bisexual, and most were encouraged by societal demands to marry. An extraordinarily large number of those like Oscar Wilde--Wilde who craved boys, craved having sex with them and watching, voyeuristically, them having sex together--married, in Oscar's case twice, and there seems to be no doubt that he had no problem in ''honoring'' both wives. Yet boys remained his preference, and he was said to have spent a total of £5,000 on Lord Alfred Douglas, who considered him his sugar daddy.
    During the Victorian Era there were far more trials against homosexuals than before 1800 because prudish Victorian police policed what was going on in Victorian bedrooms. The last person executed for homosexuality was in 1835, while the death penalty was dropped only in 1861, and became a misdemeanor in 1885, punishable by 2 years

imprisonment. From 1810 to 1835 there were 1,596 prosecutions and 46 executions.

The major symbols of male prostitution were the White Swan Scandal, the Cleveland Street Telegram Scandal and the Oscar Wilde trial, all to be discussed. Taverns existed from 1700 for male prostitution, and were called molly houses or mollies. Walter and his famous *My Secret Life* was published from 1880, in which he paid for sex with a man, ''Yes, Betsy. Get me a nice young cunt without hair on it--and a man to frig.'' And asked her to make sure he was ''no plant, Betsy,'' because the police paid informers (plants) to catch clients.

I'll mention Wilde from time to time but I won't devote a chapter to him because a brilliant man preying on uneducated lads (albeit streetwise) is of little interest to me, unless it illustrates some aspect of street trade, an example of which is Wilde's interest in Freddie Adams, 17, that he took to Paris and shared with Maurice Schwabe that Oscar picked up while there, a threesome Wilde particularly liked because as a voyeur he loved watching two youths having intercourse. Atkins was living with a blackmailer, James Burton, who had Atkins bring johns home and then walk in on them in the middle of sex. The john was blackmailed for criminally assaulting Burton's teenage ''nephew''.

A man can easily have sex daily, which adds up to potentially 300 encounters a year, but Wilde was reported as having as many as four assignations a day. The number of his boys was therefore stupendous, and those that testified during his trials stated that the average price paid was from £2 to £5. One of them admitted receiving a silver cigarette case with his name etched in it. There was a lot of fellatio and mutual masturbation, and girls were occasionally invited. Wilde favored fucking the lads, one of whom mentioned the vaseline-stiff sheets.

Wilde defended himself by asking why a man shouldn't be allowed to love a boy, rather than a woman when such was his nature. The problem was that a man of Wilde's intelligence and eloquence could make any boy surrender his ass, not a big deal, perhaps, for streetwise rent boys, but if laws hadn't existed to protect the underage one would have found Wilde and other chicken-hawks like him outside of schools.

THE WHITE SWAN SCANDAL (1810)

The White Swan was the name given to a house on Vere Street which was a major scandal of the 1800s. It was a gay club, called a molly house, in which 27 men were arrested, 6 were pilloried and 2 were hung. A total of 200 policemen were employed to protect the arrested men from mob vengeance. The house had upstairs rooms where men of position could met boys paid to service them. One of the lads was a regimental drummer of 16,

Thomas White, who would be one of the hanged. One aristocrat regularly spent a week in the house, going through as many as a dozen boys. Cooks and waiters took part, grenadiers and footmen, as well as a coal-heaver who had two handsome sons the man claimed were as degenerate as he. The boys on the premises could be ''married'' to upper-class sissies in drag, the ceremonies performed before anal intercourse. New recruits, often around age 16, were invited for dinner, put at ease, and initiated in the sex acts they were afterwards paid half a crown to perform. The house was infiltrated by the police that descended on a Sunday, the day chosen for orgies. The men were tried, receiving from 2 to 5 years imprisonment.

The men's ordeal began with their arrests, when mobs formed to scream and pound them with whatever was at hand, from rocks to mud to offal. Although protected by as many as 40 constables at a time, the miscreants were bloodied and whipped by coachmen that the police couldn't hold back.

Six were sentenced to jail and the pillory. The pillories, illustrated below, were located in Haymarket. They could hold four men at a time, whose suffering lasted an hour, during which women with baskets of fish guts, rotten eggs, human and animal dung, potatoes, pig blood and dead cats pelted them.

Pillories

When their hour was up they were led away to Newgate Prison-- encrusted with filth, knocked down, kicked and hit with objects on the way, arriving bleeding profusely.

Newgate Prison

The public at times paid with their lives, as the crowds were so dense that embankments gave way, and men and boys fell from trees and rooftops where they'd gone, as numerous as barnacles, to miss nothing of the afflictions.

One of the men who may have played a role in Thomas White's hanging was the Duke of Cumberland whose servant was apparently blackmailing him to hide the Duke's indiscretions with boys and servants like himself. The servant was found with his throat slit, and although the coroner declared he had committed suicide, there was no blood on his hands. One theory is that the duke had visited the White Swan and was White's client. Having the boy hanged was the duke's only hope of escaping scandal, especially as White may have agreed to turn the duke in in exchange for his freedom. White's mother died the day after the boy's murder, of a broken heart, wrote the *Morning Chronicle.*

THE CLEVELAND STREET TELEGRAM SCANDAL

There's an amusing angle to the Cleveland Street Telegram Scandal. Around 1889 there was a sudden increase in the number of telegrams sent between members of the aristocracy and upper classes. It eventually turned out that boys delivering them were highly amenable to exchanging sexual services for a few coins, which in a sense did no one any harm as boys are ever in need of finances to fulfill their desires, while their healthy young bodies can easily care for the sexual wishes of older men, without depleting the lads of their natural ability to ''spend'' (British for ''cum'') nearly at will (with girls, for example, later on, during the day or night, should they so wish).

But the boys were found out when the police was called in to investigate the theft of some money in a telegraph office. One of the boys working there, age 15, was searched and a personal fortune was found on him, 14 shillings, equivalent to several weeks' salary. Accused of stealing the sum from the telegraph office, the boy felt it was less damaging to tell the truth, that the money had come from gentlemen who made use of his young person.

Some of the lads.

He gave up the name of the boy, 18, who had recruited him, as well as friends who did the same as he, and added that for additional funds they all worked for a certain Charles Hammond who ran a male brothel on Cleveland Street, frequented, it was rumored, by the man who was next in line for the British throne, Prince Albert Victor, and his squire, Somerset, who fled to Paris before he could be questioned.

The concept that homosexuality was a vice practiced by nobles was reinforced when the Marquess of Queensbury's son was involved with Oscar Wilde.

A cartoon published at the time.

One of the telegraph boys warned Hammond who made an escape, avoiding a possible two-years' imprisonment.

Through his squire Somerset, a lawyer was hired, Arthur Newton, who got the boys off with 4 to 9 months of hard labor. The lawyer got money to Hammond, allowing him to install himself in America. Somerset lived out the rest of his days in the south of France, dying in 1926.

At this time in N.Y., around the Five Points, there were a reported six establishments that catered to rent boys and their johns.

The boys were young and so the question of the age of consent comes in. The age of consent is when one is permitted to have sexual relations, and has nothing to do with one's majority, which envelops the age of criminal responsibility, voting, driving and drinking.

In Ancient Greece a boy married around age 30, leaving him lots of time to play the field (although marriage did little to block him afterwards), whereas in Rome Augustus wanted his citizens to have children before age 30, and heavily fined them if they didn't, because the state was in dire need of men for wars, the running of government, for agriculture, construction, etc. Girls married around puberty or a little afterwards.

In Medieval Europe one could marry between ages 12 to 14, and in the 1500s and 1600s girls could have intercourse around age 12. After the French revolution, which abolished laws against homosexuality, intercourse was allowed at age 11, and Spain, Portugal and Denmark followed with the age of consent between ages 10 and 12.

In the 1800s the age increased to around age 13, while in the 1900s it was raised to 16 as one became aware of sexual abuse concerning girls. It went to between ages 16 and 18 in the U.S. in 1920 thanks to female reformers. Only Spain held out, allowing intercourse at age 12, and that to 1999 (!), when it increased to age 13 (!), and only in 2015 did it go to age 16, but as we all know, everything ripens faster in sunny Spain.

To my way of thinking, 16 would be perfect (although kids in the Internet Age frequently replace masturbation by intercourse around age 15).

Canada, where the age of consent is 16, allows sex between ages 14 and 15 if the partner is not more than 5 years older, and between ages 12 to 13 if the partner is less than 2 years older. The age of consent in Finland is 16, but anyone can have sex at any age if they're the same age.

Kids must nonetheless be protected from *adults* who have the power of experience, wealth and position, in which case no law can be harsh enough. (Tut-tut.)

THE SINS OF THE CITIES OF THE PLAIN

The original version of *The Sins of the Cities of the Plain* (1881) was dug up in the British Library by Wolfram Setz. The story of Jack Saul, a rent boy, began in boarding school, the sexual nursery of countless English boys, certainly the reason they are so tolerant of their sons' sexual behavior when they become parents. In Crete lads were ''abducted'' by their lovers and initiated in two months of none-stop fucking, broken with periods of the boy and his lover hunting, and the man instructing him in the art of war, a capital moment in the life of the boy, one that his father had gone through, first as a boy, then as an initiating lover himself. Saul entered a prostitution ring, had many experiences with women too, but the part of the book that had apparently attracted Oscar Wilde was Saul's school days, where we find this example:

'I was sent to a boarding-school at Colchester when about ten years of age. Here the boys all slept by twos in a bed.

'Well do I remember the first night. My bedfellow, a big boy of about fifteen, his name was Freeman, at once began to handle me all over as soon as the lights were out. His hands soon found my cock, which young as I then was, was a fine one for my age--somehow it was already stiff.

' ''My eyes,'' he whispered, ''you've got a good fun. Feel mine; it is hardly bigger than yours,'' as he directed my young hands to another equally stiff prick.

' ''Rub it up and down,'' he whispered again; ''that is what we all do. Do you like it?''

'My body was in a tremble all over, and presently, as I continued the up and down motion of my hand on his cock, it was wetted all over with a warm, slimy kind of stuff which he shot into my hand.'

The book, part fact and part fiction, includes some of the participants in The Cleveland Street Telegram Scandal.

ROGER CASEMENT
1864 – 1916

The numerous books that I read on Casement were highly sympathetic, all agreeing that Casement was tall, handsome, charming, modest, graceful, affectionate and courageous. He couldn't stand human suffering--as when African natives were put to death as human sacrifices so that a king would overcome sickness (one monarch had a thousand killed a day until he recovered) or when others were killed to serve a king in the afterlife when he died. He alerted the authorities when whites abused blacks, or Arabs sold them into slavery, and broke down in tears when an animal was hurt or one of his dogs fell ill. Yet for all the sympathy, the underlying homophobia was ever present in his biographies, as when one author--of one of the very best, most complaisant books concerning him--wrote that Casement loved to watch men at work, especially, writes the author, fine young Portuguese sailors unloading a boat, adding, ''his habit of admiring the muscular bodies of young men grows more visibly ominous as time passes.'' Would the writer have used the word *ominous* if Casement had admired a gaggle of *girls*?

Ward, left, with bearded Casement.

Engendered by intelligent parents, his father, an ardent swimmer--a form of sport Casement would love throughout his life--was in the Dragoon Guards, stationed in India. He brought up his son a Protestant and died when the boy was but 13. Casement lost his loving mother at age 9. A Catholic, it was in her faith that Casement would die, taking communion for the first and last time prior to his execution. Now an orphan, he was taken under the wing of relations and sent to Ballymena Academy where he excelled at football and tennis, history, Greek, Latin and French. It was certainly here too that he began his sexual life, as English schoolboys took their sex very seriously, and Casement, blue-eyed, handsome and 6' 2" at age 16, didn't go unnoticed. He then worked as a shipping clerk, himself shipping out for Africa at age 19, where he would spend 20 years. He met Joseph Conrad as well as other writers, one of whom wrote that Casement knew more about the Congo than any man living and ''was one of the finest men God has ever made.'' He crossed paths with Stanley too, a dark soul.

Casement's father had always been on the move, taking his children, one girl and three boys, throughout England, Ireland and Europe. Casement too would never put down his luggage in one place for long. 1889 saw him in America, the companion of Herbert Ward on a lecturing tour centered around the Congo. The handsome Ward had accompanied Stanley, who appreciated handsome boys as much as Casement, on one of his expeditions. Ward then took up sculpture and was awarded the *Légion d'Honneur* for his bravery in W.W. I. At age 15 Ward had sailed to New Zealand and then to Australia where he was a gold digger, circus performer and sail maker. His friendship with Casement lasted thirty years, and Casement was the godfather of his son. About Casement he wrote, ''Imagine a tall, handsome man, muscle and bone, a sun-tanned face, blue eyes and black curly hair. A pure Irishman with a captivating voice and singular charm.'' He fell out with Casement when Casement went to Berlin in search of arms and help in gaining Irish independence. Later, Ward refused to sign a petition circulated by Sir Arthur Conan Doyle to save Casement from execution, as did another long-term friend of Casement,

Joseph Conrad. Ward then had his son's name changed from Roger to Rodney.

Ward, for me beauty personified.

In the early 1890s Casement was back in Africa exploring and charting routes for the British Foreign Office. Part of his job was to spy on the German military active in the Congo. The Foreign Office also encouraged him to write a report on the treatment of the Congolese. This he did during a three-month trek by boat. The natives were required to supply an amount of food, as a tax, to nearby military commanders and their troops. When they didn't, they were punished. As proof of the punishment, their right hands--or even their genitals--were cut off and taken back to the authorities. Casement continually came across boys missing a hand, the rare survivors of the amputations, and others with bullet-hole scars. The Congo had ended slavery organized mostly by Arabs, but replaced it by indigenous forced labor. Looting, flogging, rape, imprisonment, mutilation and the burning of whole villages, were daily occurrences. Casement returned to Ireland in hopes that those in power, among them Joseph Conrad, would help him gain a public pulpit from which he could denounce the horrors he had witnessed.

Over the years he had traveled back and forth from Europe to Africa. Certain pages in his journal covering 1906-1916 were torn out, certainly those referring to his sexuality. A few remained. During a stopover in Madeira he rated the boys he paid by age and genital size. One boy was "youthful" and "enormous," a certain Aladdin "a splendid piece". During a trip on board the *Jebba* he got to know the sailors and serving staff. In Funchal he picked up with Perestrello, the seller of pornography. In the Old Town he had a boy "for cigarettes". He found the English lads handsome, with an air of availability. Others "delightful," "beautiful creature", "exquisite eyes". Most seemed to have been wishful longings.

One, "17 ½" allowed himself to be kissed for $4. He had already been through Las Palmas several times and had better luck as he knew where to look. On ship again he met a boy "enormous--about 18."

He learned of the death of Sir Hector Macdonald who had committed suicide in a hotel in Paris when accused of homosexuality in his former posting to Ceylon. Casement wrote in his diary that the soldier's death was terrible, and that a man shouldn't be sent to prison as a way of "curing a terrible disease." One of Casement's biographers, B.L. Reid, in his truly excellent *The Lives of Roger Casement*, wrote that a person like Casement, who suffered from the same "terrible disease," could only have written such a thing if his left hand hadn't known what his right hand was up to. But at the time it was surely impossible, given the hatred of homosexuality, to be anything but schizophrenic. In my personal case, nearly a hundred years later, I too felt that it was natural for others to be anti-gay. I made it into the Peace Corps, but only because I could convincingly lie my way through the training session, the purpose of which was to weed out undesirables like me. This is how I described the experience in my book *An American in Paris:*

Home for me was a room with three beds and two cots. It was my first experience at sharing, and I disliked it. The guys made noise until all hours, they monopolized the bathroom and they looked on me with scorn because I wouldn't take part in their pastimes: I refused to shuffle-and-giggle-and-ah-shucks-should-we? on the doorsteps of strip joints; I despised their music, their idiotic jokes and their pigskin heroes. The underlying abyss was, as always, sex. Without that common denominator we were invariably at odds. The boys farted openly, they belched like Turks, one used the can while a second pissed in the tub and a third combed his hair at the sink. Mark was as manly as any of them, and except for whom he screwed, Mark's interests were mine. We both liked music and our favorite topic was books, and we were both keen on sports: Mark competitive ones, me those made for loners, like swimming and athletics. Yet when the volunteers had their three-day battery of psychological tests, Mark came out an A-1 male while I had to go through an unexpected interview with a bulbous-nosed, toady-skinned shrink.

"Uh, the results show you like paintings, sculpture and arty things like that..." I had marked the No Interest box on any question in the least compromising; the corrector had drawn the right conclusions anyway. "Uh, you're a loner ... you know, the type that'd rather sit in the house all day sewing than toss a ball about. Now, Jamaica's a very masculine society and we're not sure if your skills (?) would go over well there..."

I jumped up and sputtered so violently I showered the shrink with spittle: "I'm no goddamned queer if that's what you're getting at, and if a guy can't like a picture you might as well shut down the goddamned museums..." The shrink stopped me with a wave of the hand and a supercilious grin and said, "Uh, that's not what I was getting at...." and changed the subject. During the mid-training deselection--based nearly solely on the shrink's report--I was left unscathed. Charlie went though. I cringed at the thought of his limp-wrist rebuttal to the same accusations. When Charlie got the word that he was no longer one of the volunteers, his jowls sagged further still, he went white, and meekly protested, "Well, why *me*?" while giving us all a look of abysmal distress. Sophie came up to help him leave the room before he broke down. He pointed a hip towards the door and followed it out. I wondered if Charlie's sacrifice--statistically there had to be at least *one* among us--had saved me. But I couldn't help wondering how the tests had shown me up and not Mark. Mark who had at least as much "sensitivity" as I, and more "arty" knowledge in his little finger, I knew, than would probably accumulate in me during my entire life. Coming as it did at the beginning of the 70s, such gay phobia didn't seem particularly unjust or even out of place to me. That I had to go through it was just too bad, *just too doggoned bad*.

In those days the Congo was of interest, with nearly daily reports on Livingston and Stanley's attempts at finding him. In London Casement reported to the Foreign Office, prepared his report, and gave interviews, content with the newspaper articles written about him and his work, all the while cruising London streets. During just one night he reported having sex with 7 men, one ''huge'' and two ''beauties''. For readers who are not gay, this activity is often par for the course for active homosexuals, the reason for which many claim to be more ''virile'' than heteros. This doesn't mean that he ''came'' with 7, but a gay's curiosity towards other boys and men in insatiable. Finishing up his report, Casement visited Joseph Conrad at his invitation for a weekend, and then proceeded to Ireland. There he found the cause and purpose of his life, Irish independence. He did wish to return to the Congo, but his report burned him as far as King Leopold II of Belgium, the Congo's sovereign, was concerned. He would never be permitted back.

The Foreign Office sent him to Santos in Brazil as consul. He found it a hole populated by mongrels. Casement could accept Africans, and even wish to return to the Congo, but he never accepted mixed-blood Brazilians, a ''muddy'' mixture of black, red and white ''swine''. He didn't stay long before moving to Pará that he found just as bad. In both places his work consisted of dealing with drunken sailors. He returned to Ireland where at Belfast strikers confronted 4,000 British troops, leaving three dead and many hurt. He took lessons in the Irish language that he felt indispensible for a future entirely free country. He was assigned to Rio, which was a far better post, but still consisted of arrogant, uncouth locals. During his travels he kept up his diary, "very deep thrusts", "up to the hilt", "deep screw to the hilt". Anal sex is a mystery to some, while to others it is the ultimate in sexual pleasure, which was Casement's case. In Rio "8 ½", young and glorious", "biggest since Lisbon", "perfectly huge", "fuck, enormous push, loved *mightily*."

I had originally planned to add a postscript in which I would reveal the contents of the Black Diaries in which he recounted his homosexual experiences, but most of the "hard" parts are already in this chapter, the rest of the entries just covers what he ate, how much to paid for his meals, the quantity of rain or fog, his fevers and complaints about mosquitoes, animals seen, plus ultra-brief sections on his chatting up boys of every social level, the cigarettes he offered, rather sad because he was apparently mostly lonely, and when active, well, to my eyes, rather demeaning.

In London he accepted a fact-finding mission to Peru where a rubber company was accused of slavery, rape, flogging, mutilation and murder. Before setting off he dined with Sir Arthur Conan Doyle, after which he strolled the night streets, having sex at 1:00 a.m. and gain at 1:45. On his way to Peru he stopped over at Madeira again, "João, splendid balls, soft, big and full, very fine one, big, long and thick".

We know volumes about Cellini thanks to his autobiography. The same is true of Casement, even if he destroyed much of the output of his diaries. Aretino left revealing letters and Machiavelli the briefest of insights, "What if he growls into the boy's ear? Don't you remember our younger years?" We know for certain that Donatello liked boys because Lorenzo de' Medici wrote to the Duke of Ferrara telling him that the sculptor was on his way to kill one of his unfaithful lovers. Luckily a single chronicler mentioned Richard I and Philippe II's sharing a bed. We know that both da Vinci and Michelangelo probably died virgin, heterosexually speaking, although in truth we have no proof that da Vinci even shared a kiss with Salaì.

In Peru Casement was accompanied by a number of fellow investigators. When they got down to their interviews some of the investigators broke down crying, including Casement. What they had heard about the beatings, torture and rapes was true. Soon the head of the rubber company said that he accepted the testimony and pleaded for the questioning to stop as it was too shocking. Even so, two of the Englishmen thought such practices were perhaps necessary in such wild, godforsaken lands; another wondered if they were not inevitable. Casement shook his head at the hesitation of such "intrinsically good men". All of them were deeply impressed by the sweetness and passivity of the Indians. The Indians were impressed by the English giants, as Casement was over six feet tall and another man was 6' 4". On a sexual level, Casement was as hypocritical as he had been when he wrote that Hector Macdonald suffered from a "terrible disease", while Casement himself thrilled at being repeatedly shafted by the deepest thrusts, as he himself wrote. Now, in the Amazon, he came upon a group of boys openly masturbating in their hammocks. He scared the lads by accusing them of beastly unchristian morality, he--if he could have gotten away with it unseen--who would have allowed the biggest, the thickest, the longest among them to send him to seventh heaven.

He and the other inspectors went inland via waterways and then trekked through forests opened up by enslaved Indians who worked without even receiving food. At the end of a fifteen-mile trek they came upon the station leader, a shock to Casement because he was not only a murderer like the others accused by the Indians, he was Irish, in perfect health, and handsome. Casement took pictures of flogging marks on the rubber carriers, one of which, that of a twelve-year-old, he wrote "a beautiful boy." His companions again tried to excuse the wounds, as they were inflicted on natives who were, after all, cannibals--which was true. Casement replied that he had dealt with cannibals in Africa, and they were fine fellows, deserving of protection.

Casement then committed what some might consider an infamy. He bought two boys to go back to England with him, bathing with both to make sure they were, as he says in his diary concerning one, "big". The boys had cost Casement a shirt and trousers, paid over to their owners. In his diary Casement said he would have Ward sculpt all three of them in bronze, stating that Ward would enjoy seeing the boys' limbs. That Casement spread his legs for all comers was one thing, that he used his authority to adopt totally uneducated boys--slaves, really--for evident sexual purposes, is something I'll leave to the reader's appreciation.

They went down the Amazon that Casement described as "the mightiest river bathing the meanest shores." He showed some pictures to the oldest of his two boys, certainly pornography, as the boy became "thick". In Pará he continued his diary: Olympio was followed immediately by Polnara and then Marco "in *deep*". He learned that the Brazilian rubber makers practiced a form of slavery as ruthless as that in Peru. In London he went to work on his Putumayo Report, the name of the Peruvian rubber site. When the report came out the *Economist* called it "masterly and horrifying" and he received a knighthood, one he wanted to decline but didn't, although Yeats had, Yeats stating that he would not sell out Ireland for a piece of ribbon. Casement learned that 215 warrants had been made out against the Peruvian slavers, but the worst escaped to neighboring Brazil. He went to Paris where he was welcomed by the models of artists friends, Dick, Nick, Denis and Pierre "enormous and fine". As inevitably happens, he was robbed in some dark park.

The Foreign Office decided to return him to Peru to prove that the British government still had its eye on what was going on there. He took his two Indian boys with him in order to return them to their rightful home. He returned via Pará "a large stiff one--long and thick and firm as a poker." The next night a man complemented him on his "much milk," his abundant ejaculation. At Manaus he let out all stops: "three times Agostinho did it and three times for two sailors, one 16--in all six times tonight."

In Quito he found out that of the 215 warrants, 9 men had been arrested. These were found not guilty and the judge who had issued the warrants was sacked. Casement turned over his two boys to friends as household servants. With nothing left to do, he returned to London via Manaus (two on Tuesday, one on Wednesday and two on Thursday).

I've skipped over Casement's illnesses. He often came down with fevers, certainly not surprising when one lived in the Congo and around the Amazon. Cold sweats. Headaches. Lead in the legs and joints, which he called rheumatism. And diarrhea. Sickness that plagued--and would continue to plague--him all his life. It must be added too that he was continually obliged to visit doctors in need of care for damage to his anus.

To enter into the politics of Ireland is a labyrinth of boggling dimensions. Just let me draw the general lines of an age-old tragedy. Protestants in the north of Ireland wished to remain with England. To ensure this, volunteers there formed an army and armed themselves. Casement and others did the same in the Catholic south. Soon the south had 100,000 volunteers and was able to import 1,500 rifles and thousands of rounds of ammunition from Germany. Casement went to N.Y., Chicago and Pennsylvania to amass funds and, because sea travel between Britain and Germany was now forbidden, to buy arms too. In N.Y. he met a 24-year-old Norwegian boy, on the make since striking out on his own at age 12, and who would play a part in Casement's life later on. His name was Eivind Adler Christensen and Casement took him under his wing. Casement was treated as a hero in America even though those who got to know him began to doubt both his tactical competence and his mental soundness. Casement met with the German ambassador and decided to sail to Germany with Christensen. He advised the ambassador to have Irish POWs in Germany united in one camp where Casement could form them into a brigade that would fight on Germany's side. In exchange, Germany promised the Irish their independence.

Eivind Adler Christensen.

In Norway an incredible event occurred. According to Christensen he was contacted by British authorities who promised him £5,000 for Casement, alive or dead (although the inclusion of "dead" may have been a Christensen invention). According to the British it was Christensen who had contacted them, offering to give up Casement for cash, revealing, at the same time, the fact that Casement and he were sleeping together, and that Casement was taking care of his financial needs. Most probably the British version was true. Bizarrely, Casement's homosexuality seemed to intrigue the authorities as much as the purpose of his trip. At any rate, they let Casement and Christensen free to go on to Berlin by train. In his diary Casement declared that Ireland "would gain from my treason." Exactly how he didn't state, since elsewhere he wrote that it was unlikely that Germany would win the war. He nonetheless wanted Germany to declare itself in favor of Irish independence.

He was warmly received in Berlin and was impressed by the serious, obedient and cheerful Germans he met on the streets, some soldiers with flowers in their belts. It was decided that he would go to Charleville in Belgium to organize an Irish Brigade, the purpose of which, suggested Casement, would be to fight alongside Germans in places like Egypt. He left Christensen in Berlin with tears in his eyes at Casement's departure, Casement wrote. In Charleville Casement was shocked by the lack of food, heating fuel and long rows of soldiers' graves. The Germans had tried to place the Irish prisoners in one location but were stymied as to how to distinguish Catholics from Protestants, Irish from Welsh, Scots and English.

Casement returned to Berlin while the German army sorted out the nationalities and religions of their prisoners. The German Foreign Office published a declaration stating that it had the best interests of the Irish at heart. This satisfied Casement and at the same time brought him to the attention of government officials in Britain and America. As for what Casement was doing on his own time: "No lack of fine, strong, handsome boys and young men," (although this was most probably more longing).

Christensen returned to Norway on various letter-carrying missions for Casement. He immediately got in touch with the British Foreign Office again, and again proposed his services for money. In Berlin Casement was warned about what Christensen was up to, but dismissed all as malicious rumors. He went to examine the Irish captives, finding them a sorry lot, dirty, miserable, "*very* wretched". Many of the Irish boys felt the Brits had placed them in the front lines during attacks, as cannon fodder. Others had been otherwise badly treated and hated the British. The problem was that they hated the Germans even more. There were 2,200 possible candidates but only two men who declared themselves willing to be members of the new Irish Brigade. Casement gave them clothes and fed them, and then sent them off to recruit others. But given the prisoners' attitude, he doubted that he would succeed. In his diary: "I used to be proud of the Irish," but after seeing the prisoners, "I am ashamed at belonging to such a contemptible race."

In Norway Christensen received word, directly from the British Foreign Office, that he would be paid £5,000 for information leading to the capture of Casement. Christensen called his British handler a supreme rascal, an accolade in Christensen's vocabulary. The handler wrote the Foreign Office that Christensen was a dangerous crook, but had promised that in addition to the £5,000 Christensen was given permission to keep any money Casement had on him that Christensen could steal prior to the arrest.

How much Casement knew of Christensen's life is unknown, but it is known that Casement was sending money to Christensen's wife. Christensen had returned home to Norway with a German girl he married, making him a bigamist. He had children by both women. Casement wrote to him, "In life and death I will never forget you and your devotion, affection and fidelity to me." Casement did manage to free 163 Irish detainees who happened to have been in Germany when war broke out, among them "one charming youth of 17, Paul O'Brian." Of the 2,200 prisoners he finally formed a Brigade of 50, which pleased the Germans as they could testify to the Brigade's existence, without referring to its size. One of them had had both legs broken when it was found out that he would fight for the Germans. As for Casement, he never returned to see the other prisoners because of their copious insults. He had nearly nothing left to do in Germany but he had nowhere else to go. He wrote to friends that he was well-known in Germany, that, in fact, he was on the lips of every householder. He claimed that he was continually turning down interviews, that a director wished to make a film of his life, and that a tobacco manufacturer wanted to bring out a cigar featuring him. It was true that at age 50 he was distinguished in his perfectly trimmed mustache and beard, and his impeccable suits. It was at this time that the *Lusitania* was sunk, bringing America into the war.

Back in Ireland plans were going ahead for independence. An Irish leader, John Devoy, had convinced the Germans to send a boat with thousands of rifles, machine guns and explosives, to be delivered before Easter Sunday, the day set for what was called the Rising. It was decided that Casement would be kept away from the action and from any decision making because the leaders felt he was incompetent, that he had put his trust in crooks like Christensen, and that he spilled the beans to absolutely anyone who took the trouble to visit him (especially if he were young and charming). Casement was to remain as an Irish representative in Germany, a kind of Irish Saint. Furious, Casement went to the Germans and insisted that they send him to Ireland by submarine so he could prepare for the landing of the weapons. When the Germans readily agreed, it dawned on Casement that they simply wanted to get rid of him once and for all. No longer wanted in Ireland, no longer wanted in Germany, Casement realized that he had been used by everyone. Everyone except the British. In his diary he wrote that he had come to the conclusion that only the British had been consistently truthful to him; that only the English were straightforward.

Casement got his wish. He entered U. 19, the same sub that had sunk the *Lusitania*. The plan was to rendezvous off the shores of Ireland with the *Aud*, a ship that carried the arms necessary for the Rising. The ship also carried a trunk with Casement's papers, his diaries, his craving for being shafted in dark alleys, pages and pages of confession that would shock and cause wild laughter behind many a closed door in the British ministries. Due to imprecise navigation, the sub and the *Aud* never met and the *Aud* was later captured. Casement and two friends came ashore in a dinghy that capsized in the rollers. Soaked, they made there way inland. Casement, deadly tired, was left in a farm outbuilding while the other two walked to a nearby town. One got away and actually was able to work his way as a fireman and coal stoker to America. The second was stopped by local police and revealed everything he knew from the moment he had been recruited in Germany, emphasizing the fact that he had joined Casement only as a way of escaping from Germany. Casement too was captured and told his entire story the moment he found himself in the presence of a presentable chap who treated him with respect, admitting even, ''I have committed treason up to the neck, not once, but a hundred times.'' Before being taken to London, to the Tower in fact, he offered as a parting gift his walking stick to one interrogator, his watch to another, his waistcoat to a third. His capture was announced in Parliament, to wild cheers, especially when the Parliamentarians were assured he would be shot, highly unsurprising given the massacre of millions on the blood-gorged fields of France.

The Rising took place, but the result was disastrous. It was set for Easter Sunday but was then delayed a day. Not everyone got news of the delay, so there was chaos when it took place. The arms hadn't arrived on the *Aud* and the arrest of Casement dampened spirits.

In the Tower Casement was left in his original clothing, now filthy, and he was soon covered with lice. Two soldiers were posted in the same room with him at all times. As he had no stomach for food he soon became cadaveric, and was threatened with being force-fed if he didn't eat more.

At first he seemed to have decided to defend himself, to incarnate Ireland for whom he was willing to die a martyr. He would go down as an Irish patriot, not an English traitor. Before the courts of the world he would defend Ireland's plea for independence. A part of him begged for death-- and he should have known that death was inevitable in his case--but another part seemed to have wanted to live, as he gave up the idea of standing alone: he accepted to be represented by lawyers. He had already hung himself a thousand times, through his letters, his interviews, his intimate confessions to any handsome interrogator who caught his eye. He had done immense good thanks to his reports on the Congo and on Peru. His defense of Ireland was certainly sincere and would succeed, in 1949, with the creation of The Republic of Ireland, which entered the United Nations in 1955. But he and his lawyers decided to refute the Crown's every accusation, one by one, which would be his undoing as he himself had proclaimed his own guilt over and over and over again. Now the argument descended to mere semantics: He said he wanted to land with German soldiers, not of German soldiers (supposedly meaning that fighting *independently* in the company of Germans for Irish freedom made him a prisoner of war, one that by law could be detained but not hanged, whereas had he fought *with* the Germans he could be tried for treason).

In Dublin those responsible for the Rising were executed. This gained the indignation of the Americans, many, many of whom were of Irish descent. An American lawyer of repute was sent to help with the defense of Casement. For Casement himself his personal comfort was vastly improving. Money was being raised for his defense, his lodgings were now correct, the food good, his hair and beard trimmed, his clothes again impeccable, and he received so many visits from family and friends that he could even offer himself the luxury of turning away ministers due to his lack of time.

The trial went on but the result was forgone. Millions dead on the battlefields of Europe, a horrid number of them British, a knighted hero now a pariah. Found guilty of treason, Conan Doyle was the first to come forward with a plea and petition for clemency, emphasizing Casement's poor mental health and disapproval in America should he be executed. George Bernard Shaw wrote an article stating that Casement should indeed be hanged, not for treason, but for having been born an Irishman.

His former friend Ward in Paris refused to answer Casement's pleas to get in contact with him, understandable, perhaps, because one of Ward's sons, a captain, was killed at Neuve Chapelle. A second, a pilote, was shot down, taken prisoner, and then escaped to Switzerland. Ward turned one of his homes into a French hospital, received the *Croix de Guerre*, and died from war-related injuries. The name of his third son, as related, was changed from Roger Casement Ward to plain Roddie. One leader maintained that after Casement's death as much of the diaries as decency allowed should be published, and wondered if Conan Doyle would be in his favor if he knew what Casement had done after one of their dinners together. His rent boy Christensen disappeared from the pages of History.

Casement's warders were said to have been kind, and Casement was calm. He decided to convert to his mother's religion, Catholicism. A priest came to instruct him in his new faith when, incredibly, Casement remember having water splashed over him as a baby. Registers were checked and proof of his baptism found. He took the sacraments for the first time in his life, refused food so as not to contaminate the Host, and was hanged.

MODERN TIMES

JACQUES D'ADELSWÄRD-FERSEN
1880 - 1923

During the time of Jacques d'Adelswärd-Fersen (whom I'll call Fersen from herein), rich boys often turned to writing poetry to justify their existence, something Byron did, something the wealthiest English commoner, Thomas Beckford did, both of whom have a very important place in this book. It is extremely difficult to judge their works because in modern times we need a Rosetta Stone to understand what they were trying to reveal to us. The basis for the obscurity were the laws of the land, so severe that one could be pilloried or hanged by the neck until dead, an excellent reason to encipher one's thoughts and lusts. In comparison, the texts from Ancient Greece, 2000 years earlier, are as clear as sparkling Spartan mountain cascades. Fersen was lucky in that France had given up burning boy-lovers since 1791, following the French Revolution, but one was nonetheless forbidden to incite boys to debauch or to debauch minors. There were also laws against public indecency, laws that were diverted to cover whatever the police wanted them to cover. The police in Paris used these provisions of the law as an excuse to raid taverns, brothels, parks, and other hangouts of sexual adventure, open to the public. Scandal was an ever-hazardous threat, and nobody, absolutely nobody, wanted to be accused of vile sodomy, especially not when one was a noble, or the head of a family, or the father of children, or the director of a factory or enterprise.

Friedrich Alfred Krupp committed suicide when denounced by a male servant, and there was always a disgruntled valet or chauffer or stable boy willing to turn against his employer if not richly paid off, not to speak of rent boys who made a living out of blackmail, boys men turned to because the thirst for boy sex was inexhaustible and relentless, then as today.

Fersen

The hic in the case of Fersen, as in that of Byron and Beckford, was that their tastes for boys dated back to boarding-school dormitories, and the remembrance of fresh, young, often virgin bodies, a taste that frequently increased as one aged. While anything was permissible in schools among students, having sex was as illegal then as it is today when adults were involved, and rightly so as boys must at all cost be protected from adult enticements, as well as from highly experienced predators. In Renaissance Florence boys were bought on the street from age 9, which was also against the law but so prevalent that the adult offender got off with a fine (unless the boy was forced, in which case men could be--and at times were--burned alive).

Born in Paris in 1880, Fersen's grandfather, a Swedish count, founded a steel industry at Longwy in the east of France, which Fersen inherited at age 22, his father having died at age 40, perhaps of yellow fever contracted in Panama, when Fersen was seven. Fersen had a brother, Renold, who died young. Both father and brother were greatly loved by Fersen, if one can judge from the characters in his books, often named Axel after his father, and Renold. Fersen went to Science-Po in Paris, its best school then as today, and the University of Geneva. His literary reputation resides on his oeuvre, ten collections of poems, three novels and the creation of a literary review called *Akademos*.

Fersen

His best friend and lover was Hans de Warren, a school chum with whom he would pickup boys, often directly as they left their *lycées*, at times in parks. The lads were invited home to Fersen's wealthy residence near the Arc de Triomphe after a joyride in the family royal-blue Darracq, driven by a liveried chauffeur. There the boys would be offered cakes and wine, shown Fersen and Warren's extensive collection of pornography, and, thus excited, they would be masturbated and blown. There is no record of anal sex, but the subject would have been avoided even by later police investigators, or referred to in such general terms as to make denial easy, to the relief of the offenders and the questioners. One of the boys confessed that Fersen drew a picture of his penis, and he measured that of another, hard. A third lad said that after inhaling ether and ingesting morphine, Fersen, misty-eyed, proposed that they both go to Venice where he would give the boy half his fortune, and where they would die in a suicide pact.

All of this came out after the incident that brought both Fersen and Warren to trial. Both boys, in their early twenties, organized living tableaux that they put on in front of an audience. The actors in the tableaux were all young boys, from age 7 to 17, the average age being 14. The seven-year-old had an extremely early sexual awakening, thanks to his brothers who were participants, and whose talk and nightly masturbation filled him in on adolescent sex. During the tableaux the boys took poses while poetry was read. The boys, as well as the audience, were made up of the crème of Parisian society, the boys coming from the very best families and schools, the audience being formed of men--but some women--estimated as being 70% pederastic. During the tableaux one of the boys would always be naked, his privates covered by gauze if seen frontally, his buttock *au naturel* if lying on a couch or the floor. Afterwards they would retire to the bathroom to clean up. Aroused by their performance, they gratefully allowed the two older boys to masturbate and blow them. Fersen and Warren would also allow themselves to be manipulated until ejaculation.

The séances went on twice a week, Thursdays and Sundays, until the father of the seven-year-old found out and demanded that the police arrest

Fersen and Warren, threatening, when they hesitated because of the families involved, to go public if they didn't. They did, but he went public anyway, and the resultant scandal was horrendous. The seven-year-old and his two brothers must have gone through hell at the hand of their daddy, but of this we know nothing.

Fersen was examined by three psychiatrists, one of which *purportedly* diagnosed him with inherited insanity, alcoholism and epilepsy. A physician, Doctor Socquet, found he had scabies (a contagious skin infection caused by mites) and gonorrhea, and the judge questioning him *and* his clerk were said to have gone to public baths after each interrogation to avoid contamination (private bathrooms in one's apartment were still rare at the time).

A fictional account of the tableaux, called Black Masses in the press, came out in 1904, written by the pornographer Alphonse Gallais, *Les Mémoires du Baron Jacques*, in which Baron Jacque's mother takes his virginity at an early age (Byron lost his to a maid at age 9). Baron Jacques goes on to deflower his own young boys, copulating with them on his mother's skeleton!

For Fersen's times what he did was highly titillating, and because minors were involved he was sentenced to five months in prison. As he was no longer welcome by family and friends, he exchanged Paris' cloudy skies for sunny Capri. But before we get to his exploits there, perhaps a word on his oeuvre.

In 1902 he published a collection of poems called *L'Hymnaire d'Adonis*, in which we find the poem *Treize Ans*: At age 13, blond with precocious eyes full of desire and emotion, his lips already street wise, he's in the study hall where all the boys are reading, bent over their books, while only he, in a corner, is going through randy poems by Musset. As the supervisor goes by he hides what he's doing and pretends to be hard at work, but when the coast's clear he brings out his book and, turning into the shadows so as not to be seen, he slips his hand into his pocket where a hole leads to his toy that, lost in licentious thoughts, he fondles for a long, long time. (*Treize ans, blondin aux yeux précoces, Qui disent le désir et l'émoi, Lèvres, ayant je ne sais quoi De mutin, de vicieux, de gosse. Il lit; dans la salle ils sont Tous penchés à écrire un thème, Lui seul dans un coin lit quand même, Des vers de Musset, polissons; Le pion passe, vite il se cache, Semblant travailler avec feu, À quelque devoir nébuleux, Très propre, soigné et sans tache, Puis calmé, le moment d'après, Reprend tout rose sa lecture, Se met à changer de posture, Pour être de l'ombre plus près; Coule ses mains, sans qu'on devine, Dans sa poche percée d'un trou, Et là longuement fait joujou, Rêveur de voluptés félines!*)

As you learn in the chapter on Byron, sex was a daily and nightly pastime in boarding schools. Besides his school experiences, Fersen is known to have loved a young British boy from Eton during a summer holiday on the island of Jersey.

In 1904 he wrote a novel entitled *Lord Lillian*, which is about his trial and is dedicated to the judge that collected the information (in France a single judge collects facts for-and-against a person accused of a crime, and is supposed to present the facts, neutrally, to the court. This neutrality rarely takes place and is the cause of hundreds of years of injustice, but the power of the judiciary is such that a new system cannot be adopted).

The main character in Fersen's book is Renold, Lord Lyllian (named after his brother), who lost his adulterous mother and beloved father before the age of 17. He falls into the hands of a certain Skilde (Oscar Wilde), the author of *The Portrait of Miriam Green* (*Dorian Grey*). Skilde farms the boy out to take care of the sexual needs of Skilde's clients but following the suicide of a member of one of Skilde's orgies he flees, while Skilde is imprisoned and condemned to hard labor.

Renold tours the world, going from lover to lover until he meets a Swedish poet Axel Ansen (Axel from his father's name) who unfortunately dies young. Renold goes to Paris where he creates Black Masses with naked choirboys, one of which dies. Fersen has Renold proclaim that the Masses were simply to excite the boys so that they would find shared love among themselves (which is certainly what happened in the case of Fersen in his real life in Paris). Fersen is thought to have put himself into four of his characters, all of which make love together at some point in the novel, and of course his greatest sexual partner was the poet Axel.

Renold decides to give up boy-love and marries a girl. In real life Fersen had been on the verge of marrying a very rich young lady who, despite his begging to see her, refused him following his trial.

His book *Youth* was dedicated to his very young lover Nino Cesarini, "More beautiful than the light of Rome."

It concerns the painter Robert, age 23, who is in love with Nino, a 16-year-old seminary student. But a priest is also in love with Nino *and* a girl, a girl Nino is in love with. Finally, the girl dies and Nino himself becomes a priest.

He wrote a poem entitled *So Sang Marsyas* which related the true story of his belovèd Nino who, in Venice, met and appreciated a girl, Alexandrine, who liked him so much she followed him to Capri where he bedded her. In the poem Fersen asked, "How many tears must I shed to wash away her kisses?"

In 1909 he published 12 editions of a cultural magazine called

Akademos, a total of 2,000 pages, that was said to have been about 10% homosexual. It failed after a year.

Le baiser de Narcisse, The Kiss of Narcissus: Again, due to the times, one was cautious in what one wrote, especially if one wished a wide audience. In this book the most daring sentence evokes the hero coming upon a group of youths, whose tunics of transparent linen revealed their young and muscular forms.

"Extremely young, he undid his tunic that he let fall to the ground, and in a pose equal to that of a god, he remained still, while the sun spread its golden rays over the mother-of-pearl forms of his flesh. His muscular legs rose like two columns of alabaster to his flat stomach and his precocious virility. He then sang and danced, in his glorious nudity."

The boy in question was Milès, born in Bithynia, the birthplace of Antinous. As a child he was already so beautiful that people turned to watch him pass, "for in those times the people knew how to appreciate beauty and a boy's splendid forms, a time before Antinous, born to please an emperor, and they all exclaimed, This boy is for Zeus, for they knew of the gods' love for earthlings."

The boy is taken as a slave to Athens by the architect Scopas who falls in love with him and frees him but is not given the boy's love in return, and so he dies of despair. The lad, by then 15, poses for the painter Ictinos for a fresco of Ganymede, Zeus' love mate. Milès then travels until he comes to a pond into which he finally sees a boy as beautiful as he. He leans over to kiss the image, his fingers slip … and the book ends.

Now back to Fersen's life.

Rich but rejected, he withdrew to Capri, noted for being a homosexual refuge since Tiberius withdrew there 2000 years previously. Fersen built a palace, the Villa Lysis, facing Tiberius' Villa Jovis, a neoclassical affair of Ionic columns, an entrance with an atrium, and bedrooms with wondrous views of the palace gardens, the distant sea and Mount Vesuvius. There he surrounded himself with island boys until he was requested to leave when he brought in boys from elsewhere, in competition with the homegrown crop, a loss of income for the lads and their families. The Caprian boys in question have been immortalized by a succession of photographers and painters, their bodies caressed by generations of financially fortunate lovers of boys.

A basement apartment, called the Chinese Room, was dedicated to opium smoking, where Fersen contented himself with up to 40 pipes a day, a huge but supposedly not unheard of quantity for addicts. Opium depresses the urge to have sex, although it can be used to postpone an orgasm, allowing more enjoyment before eventual ejaculation. Taking 40 pipes meant he was having no orgasms at all. It was in the Chinese Room that, in 1923, at age 43, his health failing, he drank a mortal cocktail of cocaine and champagne, certainly entering eternity with an ecstatic Wow!

But we haven't quite reached that point in his life story.

The villa completed, Fersen went off on one of several trips to India and China from where he returned with his baggage full of opium and his head imbued with Hinduism. Because he had been ostracized from Capri, he went to Rome where he met the 14-year-old Nino Casarini, the love of his life, whom he worshipped, as did Hadrian with Antinous, by having the boy immortalized in paintings, sculptures and photos by the greatest homosexual artists of the times, Umberto Brunelleschi, Francesco Ierace, Guglielmo Plüschow and Paul Höcker. With Nino in tow, he returned to the Orient.

He was able to return to Capri, perhaps because he took on more Caprian boys to care for his villa and grounds, but immediately earned a second ostracism when he published, in 1909, *And the Fire was Extinguished by the Sea*, a tell-all about the mores and quirks of the inhabitants, who recognized themselves. But thanks to his sister, who had married into Roman nobility, he was able to return where, like Tiberius, there were said to have been nightly orgies in his villa and in local grottos. He was again requested to leave, this time from Italy itself.

Back in Paris he began the magazine *Akademos*, already described. He and Nino became habitués of Parisian gay clubs, which, I can assure the reader from my own experience, had absolutely nothing of the excitement that went on, later in N.Y., at Studio 54. In 1910 Nino, drunk, grievously hurt a young cyclist at the wheel of Fersen's automobile. Both then left for Nice and Porquerolles, a nice town and a beautiful island. Nino was obliged to do his military service, after which he returned to Capri where he and Fersen were still again admitted. Fersen spent a great deal of his time in what a newspaper called his Opiarium. In 1920 he met 15-year-old Corrado Annicelli, the son of a notary on vacation on the island.

Nino

It's true that life is an eternal recommencement, varying only in details, and here too Fersen was lead by the nose by a boy, exactly as Byron had surrendered, at the end of his life, to a 15-year-old Greek lad. Fersen's boy is said to have extracted every gift he could wish for from Fersen, but in the end the boy seems to have genuinely grown to love the man, a lucky break Byron was not to know. The boy certainly had little sexual contact with Fersen, impotent from his opium and cocaine, and Fersen most probably contented himself with gazing at the lad's nudity.

The part played by Nino at the time is not known, although he was there, chauffering man and boy, and he even went to Naples to bring Fersen back to Capri, accompanied by Corrado, when Fersen was too sick to return unaided.

There he committed suicide, a gold coin was placed on his tongue to pay Charon for his passage over the River Styx, and he was cremated.

Corrado went on to become an appreciated Italian actor. He died in 1984.

Nino received shares in the Longwy steel mills, the money Fersen had in his bank accounts, and any money found in the Villa Lysis, a strange provision we find in the life of Roger Casement where his lover too had been allowed to keep any money he could extract from Casement at the time of his execution. Nino had the right to live in the villa until his death. Instead, he went to Rome where he bought a kiosk and opened a bar. He died in 1943.

AMERICA 1920s

BERLIN 1930s

Bill Tilden was the first American to win the Wimbledon men's championship, in 1920. He was also one of the saddest men to have lived. Perhaps due to his homosexuality he was isolated, as no other known homosexual athletes ever went so far as he did, winning, during six long years, every tournament he played in, conquering ever title. He couldn't stand crowds unless playing tennis in front of them, and his biographer, Frank Ford in his superb *Big Bill Tilden*, says, ''It's quite likely that in his whole life Tilden never spent a night alone with an adult, man or woman.'' He would spend many, though, with boys. Until he was on the downhill he was thought to have sublimated his sexual urges in his playing before his admirers. Afterwards he gave his full attention to schoolboys, on whom he lavished time, money and gifts. He coached them in tennis if they were so oriented. We have pictures of two such lads, and they were gorgeous. Gorgeous Tilden himself never was, but commanding, yes. At 6' 1'' he was thin and angular, and gave off the arrogance of the extremely lonely. He could be admired but never loved by the public, he was too formal for that, too unbending, and, again, too *angular*.

Big Bill

He won Wimbledon at age 27, extremely late for an athlete, and was invincible until age 33. He deemed himself an intellectual and tried to give his audience a show, letting lesser players win the first few sets before coming in for the kill. He even wrote a book on the subject, *The Art of Tennis*. He made the rounds as player and then coach until felled by cardiac arrest, a different boy in every port, but he died as he had lived, totally alone, because the boys grew into men--Tilden never. Tilden was Peter Pan.

1920 tennis, compared to manly football, basketball and baseball, was an upper-class sissy's game, with men decked out in white flannel trousers and white oxford shirts, shaking hands with one's opponent and the chair umpire, courteous and a good loser. Tilden had been born into a wealthy family, had lived in the family mansion, and had been a member of clubs catering to his class of Brahmans. The requirement for success in tennis was a millionaire daddy.

Men found him fruity, raising knowing eyebrows, as confident heterosexuals invariably do, when he minced past. Women found him attractive, but then women have a different agenda. He never displayed himself naked in the locker room, a situation tennis players could get away with if they so wished, and although immaculate on the courts, he was said to have been less hygienic off. He was also a chain smoker, although some claim he never inhaled.

Whether he had sex before he was over-the-hill is unknown, but given his rate of seduction in later years, it was highly probable. His boys were treated with outlandish generosity. They were literally forbidden to spend a dime. Room service in hotels and hotel boutiques were at the boys' entire disposal--they only had to sign his name for whatever they wanted, a disposition that existed during that far-away time. One boy stole $400 from his wallet, an immense sum then, and Tilden's reaction was to laugh it off over lunch with a friend, apparently proud of the boy's initiative. There is reason to believe that he truly loved each and everyone, and truly harbored plans to make them tennis greats.

He stayed in the best hotels and, thanks to his years of predominance, knew absolutely everyone. He especially loved junior tournaments, putting in an appearance during the dinners to honor the young tennis players. He turned professional and, thanks to his fame, mounted his own tournaments. As he neared forty he became more relaxed about his sexuality. He traveled with his ball boys of whom he had an inexhaustible source. He preferred German ball boys, taught to stand at attention when he came on the court. He was especially fond of pre-war Berlin in which homosexuality was totally open. The Germans were Tilden fans and the police protected his every move. Everyone on the tennis circuit knew about his sexuality and could break his game by deliberately imitating his effeminate gestures, gestures that were becoming increasingly evident as he aged. No scandals broke out at that time, but he was rumored to have paid to keep certain of his indiscretions quiet, notably on trains.

Tilden coached Gottfried Cramm during a Davis Cup championship against Americans. How close they were is unknown. What is known is that Cramm admitted to a three-year-long love affair with Manasse Herest, for which the Nazis sent him to prison for a year. The great American tennis man Don Budge had a petition sent to Hitler, which may have been responsible for a reduced sentence of six months.

Gottfried Cramm   Cramm with Don Budge

Cramm was a paradigm for several reasons. He was genuinely loved for his fair play and gentlemanly conduct. He won the French Open twice and was ranked the world's #1 player in 1937. He was also gorgeous, so Aryan-looking that the Nazis begged him for his support, which he refused. In 1977 he won entry into the International Tennis Hall of Fame. Later in life he became a businessman and was killed when his car ran head-on with a truck in Cairo.

A sterling boy in every sense, he is one of the rare, entirely undisputed heroes of this book.

Cramm against Lacoste, nicknamed the Crocodile.

Tilden and Cramm went bar hopping in Berlin, the world capital of homosexual sex and available rent boys. This affords us a chance to have a look at sex through recent history in general, and in Berlin in particular.

Cramm

What is amazing in the history of love among males was that after the Renaissance there followed an age darker than the Middle Ages that had preceded the Renaissance. Love between males during the Renaissance could be punished by death, but in reality under Lorenzo *Il Magnifico* de' Medici one got off with a simple slap on the hand. No one was punished because everyone was doing it. All males participated at some point in their lives in sharing an orgasm with another male. As girls were worth their weight in gold thanks to advantageous marriages that would enrich their husbands, they were kept locked away in Brinks-like security. Unlike a boy who could offer himself to a hundred passing hands or mouths or anuses and still claim innocence, a girl had one chance, after which the fruit was eternally spoiled.

After the Renaissance we stepped back into the dark, where lads, in the 1800s, could not comprehend their attraction to lads, those they had seen swimming in rivers and lakes, naked and so beautiful the boys dreaming of them inundated their own bellies in equally wondrous rivers and lakes. Till then, men were thought to have become homosexuals because they were so insatiable sexually that they simply turned to men as an alternative to women who now bored them. To keep boys on the right track laws were harsh, although thankfully the death penalty had been dropped, except, in one of life's never-ending paradoxes, in Berlin--until 1868. It was felt that men who cared for other men were in reality women trapped in a man's body, which would not only account for their searching out other men, but would account too for those like Tilden who were effeminate. The woman within was seeking an outlet for her femininity.

Men who were lucky, mostly educated men who emigrated to places like Berlin, could find sexual satisfaction in the garrison city of 400,000 where soldiers padded their pay by selling themselves, and that for generations. The unlucky ones, the vast majority, may have felt that they and their sexuality were alone in the world, that no others shared their dreams and lust. These would live and die alone. It is only here and now, 200 years later, in rare places like France where I live and will live out my days, that one can now marry the boy of one's choice. Indeed, following the French Revolution laws against sodomy were abolished in France in 1791. Under French influence, they were abolished also in Spain, Belgium, the Netherlands and Italy. Certain parts of Germany followed. In Bavaria, for example, only those who raped other men or who had sex with boys under 12 were prosecuted. But in all parts of Germany men could be imprisoned if they did something against public decency, a seemingly normal demand since having sex, for example, in the middle of a public street (homosexual or heterosexual sex), struck everyone as bad form. The law, in reality however, was diverted to cover whatever the police wanted it to cover. An example: a boy who related to another boy how he had been fucked--but well paid--in a park, was overheard by a woman who was shocked, a public act of indecency because the boys had spoken in public. The man was found and jailed. But even this liberalism was revoked following several horrendous rapes of minors, and in 1871 laws were again reenacted in Germany against sodomy.

The population of Berlin exploded, from the 400,000 mentioned to 4 million in 1920. Berlin went from a city of open sewers to the first city ever electrified, with, in 1800, electric streetcars and lighting. It went from a city of open sewers to one of public toilets and baths, from the filthiest to the cleanest city in the world, infinitely more hygienic than London, Paris and N.Y. At the end of the 1400s in Florence the Office of the Night was formed to put an end to sodomy. The penalty was death but, as stated above, everyone got off with a slap on the wrist, except those who forced children to have sex. In 1885, Berlin established the Department of Homosexuals, proof of the growing number of gays. The police collected information and mug shots of homosexuals, and encouraged doctors and educators to study Berlin's unique sexual subculture, thanks to which reams of information concerning the sexuality of the times have come to us. In 1896 the name of the Department of Homosexuals was changed to Department of Homosexuals and Blackmailers. More money could be gained by pimps putting 14-year-old boys on the streets and then blackmailing the clients. In 1902 Friedrich Alfred Krupp, the Cannon King, committed suicide when blackmail led to the publication of his preference for Italian boys. For such a rich, powerful man to end his own life so young spoke volumes about being branded a homosexual, about the prevalence of blackmail and about the availability of underage lads. The department store magnate Hermann Israel killed himself on his yacht at age 40 when his companion blackmailed him. Before dying Israel turned the boy's threatening letters over to the police. The lad was sentences to two months imprisonment. Victims of blackmail numbered in the hundreds, two of whom were well-known jurists, one who shot his blackmailer when he literally didn't have a cent left to pay him off. In 1902 a 28-year-old ophthalmologist committed suicide when his card was found in a boy's jacket and the ophthalmologist was threatened with a trial. At the time, it was established that a third of Berlin's homosexuals were being blackmailed. But as Berlin's reputation for male prostitution bloomed, johns from all over Europe flocked to the world's greatest center of boys.

Kiosks were literally flooded with dozens of publications, and the kiosk owners didn't hesitate to have some pinned open, showing nude males. In 1930 Berlin had 280,000 tourists a year, among which were 40,000 Americans. There were believed to have been 100,000 rent boys, all out for money to live on or pocket change, 1/3 were believed to have been heterosexual. And they were cheap, especially soldiers going for 50 pfennig. Thomas Mann discovered Berlin at age 17, and two other noted writers were Christopher Isherwood who wrote ''Berlin means boys'' and W.H. Auden. Isherwood refused to pay more than 10 marks, dinner and a few drinks for his boys (although this was outrageously overpaying), W.H. Auden, in his diary, detailed all sexual encounters, and the architect Philip Johnson claimed to have learned German through the horizontal method.

Isherwood and his boys (out of a purported 500).

Neither minors nor anyone badly dressed were admitted to the clubs in west Berlin. In the east everyone could enter. The sex was wildly tame compared to today's backrooms. At the urinals boys showed their wares, and at tables boys allowed johns to put their hands through their pockets, which had been cut away inside to allow seizure of the boys' dicks. Isherwood was said to have had 500. Today, boys can do that in a year, easily. But here we're talking about quantity. Quality is a completely different story. Scotty Bowers in his fascinating book *Full Service* relates that heterosexuals who requested his services rarely asked for more than a redhead or big tits, while homosexuals were extremely demanding (see Bowers in chapter on actors). And it's true. That was the problem in Berlin. The beautiful boys were in private clubs and in private hands, wealthy hands, hands that could offer far more than Isherwood's ten marks, even if ten marks were extremely generous for what was available. The boys who went with Isherwood thought he was fabulously rich because they were fabulously lacking in the attributes that would place them in an entirely different class.

Then, as today, coke was ubiquitous, except that it had just been invented, by Albert Niemann, and was not only full accepted, it was recommended by Freud to his patients.

With the arrival of the Nazis and the destruction of Röhm things came to an instant halt. 100,000 men were found guilty of homosexual crimes and between 5,000 to 15,000 died in camps, terrible but far fewer than I had imagined.

Today the legal age of consent is 16 in Germany, which strikes me as imminently justifiable.

As Tilden's arrogance increased he lost all popularity among American spectators, and twice chair umpires left the court because they couldn't stomach him anymore.

In later years Tilden told psychiatrists named to judge his mental condition that he had started having sex at age 10 with another boy of 10, petting until years later both could ejaculate, which they did my mutual manipulation. He said too that at the University of Pennsylvania he had had a friend with whom he petted and brought off with his hand. Frank Deford relates that during the French championships of 1927 French reporters, in the know, paid a boy to proposition Tilden, but Tilden did no more than fondle the kid's dick while he remained fully clothed--not enough, apparently, to merit being exposed in the French press.

Later Tilden coached Sandy Weiner, a supremely beautiful boy, whom he took with him when he gave lessons to the likes of Charley Chaplin and Douglas Fairbanks (not the exquisite Douglas Fairbanks Jr.) Then one fall Sandy just decided to go out for football and dropped tennis. Tilden had been totally devoted to the boy until, later, he was replaced by Arthur Anderson. For understandable reasons homosexuals are the very best teachers because their interest in their acolytes is absolute. Caring for a boy's education is the Platonic and Socratic ideal, although Tilden, just like the hypocritical Plato and Socrates (who claimed their interest was Platonic only), went all the way--kissing, petting, mutual jerking--if the occasion presented itself. To this both Plato and Socrates added anal intercourse when and where they could (see my book *Greek Homosexuality*). Naturally, far from all of Tilden's boys, those he coached, had sex with him, but most recognized, afterwards, that the sex angle was always present.

Sandy Weiner

As stated, Tilden came across Arthur Anderson (no photo available) when the boy was 10 and, impressed by his seriousness, offered the lad free tennis lessons. This is a perfect copy-and-paste of da Vinci who came across Salaì at age 10 and, impressed by the boy's drawings, bought him from his poor parents. Arthur too was poor, a boy who lost his father to alcohol. Tilden paid the rent for him and his mother. Arthur eventually climbed to #17 in America, not bad in a nation of hundreds of millions.

At the age of 50 Tilden was appointed head of the Professional Tennis Players Association, thanks to his name. In 1946, while driving through Beverly Hills, his car, swerving erratically along Sunset Boulevard, was pulled over by the police because it seemed obvious that Tilden was preoccupied with a lad's trousers. When the car came to a stop four of the boy's fly buttons were found open.

Tilden pleaded guilty and when jailed asked for a lawyer. Tilden told the lawyer to stifle the affair as all the others had been stifled in the States and England. But Tilden was indicted. The lawyers found out that the boy was 14, had learned everything there was to know about sex in his private school, and had already screwed a girl earlier in the day, bragging to Tilden that he had indeed been keeping himself busy (while fondling the lad Tilden had tried to find out everything he knew about sex and, said the boy, was duly impressed by his experience). The only way that could be found to free Tilden was by giving him professional psychiatric help. This was done but Tilden hanged himself by telling the judge that he had never touched a boy before. There was no proof to the contrary, but everyone knew he had been chasing boys and having sex with them for years. The judge was said to have turned red before the outrageous lie. Tilden was therefore sentenced to year in prison.

The Florence of da Vinci, Cellini and Varchi, where lads spread their legs at age 10, was gone. Other times, other mores. The absolute priority today must be the protection of boys. What lads do among themselves is their own business. If adults try to sexually--or otherwise--abuse them, they must be punished. Tilden is a rare case in which someone rich and famous didn't get off scot-free.

He used the time in jail to write *My Story*, silly, self-serving nonsense. Arthur Anderson and his mother stood by him, as did Chaplin. Released early for good behavior, he resumed touring schools for boys. He picked up a certain Michael who reported him to the police. Tilden had opened Michael's fly and introduced his hand. When repulsed, Tilden simply did it again, and then again. Chaplin offered to take him "in custody" but such recourse didn't exist under the law. Tilden again lied, but Michael's controlled testimony nailed him. He was sent back to jail.

By now he was a pariah. Chaplin had left the country, this time definitively. Never the cleanest of persons, now Tilden let himself go completely. His father had lived 60 years and 140 days. Tilden too died of a heart attack at 60 years and 117 days.

ESCORT SERVICES

Personally I can't see the interest of online Escort Services. I need to talk to a boy. To see his degree of masculinity. His intelligence. If he's straightforward or if he avoids eye contract. How he moves. He has to turn me on, and this a fellow just can't know through a picture or telephone call or an exchange of emails. A week ago (it's August here in Hossegor in France where I'm now writing this, on my sailboat) I met a boy on the quay overlooking the Port of Capbreton. Sublime. I've never seen such perfect teeth, plus a slight mustache that was a wonder. Great body, and what looked like a marble-solid ass. I gave him my email and, leaving, a first physical contact through a handshake, one so dead-fish and wimpy that there was no possibility of meeting him again, even though I was willing for him to be my very first hustler. It reminded me of an encounter I'd had in Myconos. I'd rented a house and invited back a gorgeous English boy. I shucked my clothes and waited for him, naked in bed, while he slowly undressed, something I adore watching. Then suddenly he began to tell me about the *dress* his mother was making him for some up-coming party in London. My hard-on deflated, I pretended to have a sudden and urgent problem due to something I'd eaten, and showed him out.

As I've mentioned elsewhere, the boys advertised on Escort Services simply are not physically up to par. As I'm writing this, boat after boat is going by, the French lads heartbreakingly beautiful. But not a single gay among them, because the usual 10% of the gay portion of humanity does not come to this part of France, a surfer's paradise, a boy heaven. But straight. Nothing equivalent to these lads can be found on an Escort site.

That's why I was contemplating paying. It was the only way I'd find a little company with the kid I'd met on the quay, obviously straight too, but one I'd have pulled out all stops to please--if the handshake hadn't told me he'd be as sexually exciting as making love to an ironing board.

In a word, it's all based on lust--with a faint hope of love, or understanding, or *something* more than a shared orgasm.

Escort rendezvous can be unsafe, of course, for both participants, as people are beaten up and murdered, far more often, I would suspect, than is reported to the police or by the newspapers. And drugs are often involved to help the rent boy get through what he has to do to make a few bucks. The guy paying is rarely happy being obliged to do so, and finally, there is *always* the possibility of contracting a fatal disease.

Smart escorts wear a condom, some even when giving blowjobs. They have regular physical examinations, and they refuse to be tied up. Escorts often try their hands at modeling and acting, a part of their sexual expertise coming from casting couches. Escort sites give a boy's height, weight, waist size and length of cock. Sometimes his ''gayness'' is revealed, one boy saying he was 94.6 % gay! What they'll do sexually is occasionally mention, as is their insistence or not on condoms. Some rent boys make a distinction between themselves and hustlers who try to milk every cent from a client, and don't hesitate to use force. How much they make varies wildly, sums from $1,000 a week to $30,000 when they go abroad, and there's a natural tendency to exaggerate one's importance by vastly exaggerating the amounts made.

Besides all the dangers already mentioned, there's one surprising draw back. Men fall in love with rent boys, which is an immense ordeal because the boys have a very, *very* limited time to build up a nest egg and can't be reined in by love. That said, some boys, often the most sexually exciting, do drop out of sight, perhaps, as we see in the section on the book *Full Service*, because they're taken in by rich, often super rich, lovers. I *imagine* there's some kind of contract for the boy, an offer he can't refuse. The rent boy, too, sometimes falls in love, which seems to work, for a time at least, between boys who do the same work and are around the same age. Otherwise it's a burden. There's probably a lot of stress in such relationships, and a lad who sees multiple clients a day--most demanding that he ejaculate--must leave both boys with little more than friendly warmth and a loving presence to offer (which of itself is a lot).

Escort Services earn a fee for booking and expediting their boys, and the boys pay either a fixed price for setting up a date or a percentage of what the date brings in. The rest is left up to the boy, although the client is forewarned of the price. Some Escort Agencies really do provide just escorts, without sexual services, but they're probably extremely rare. Many Escort Services keep close tabs on their boys, having them call in the moment they arrive at their destination. Clients call agencies and describe their needs, and the agency suggests an appropriate lad. Agencies arrange rendezvous so that their boys have complete anonymity. Services are incall, at the rent-boy's home, or outcall, at a hotel or the client's home. Some boys advertise in papers without going through an agency.

A young hustler was recently interviewed, and he brought up some of these aspects: He was a highly intelligent straight boy who began work in the sex trade by appearing in Live Sex Shows in which he had intercourse with his girlfriend. It was exciting for him, performing in front of an audience, and an enormous adrenaline rush. Although he was making what he called huge amounts of money, he had free time he used as a prostitute for men, as women rarely paid for an escort. His clients were over 50 and although he rarely had intercourse, when it took place he was the bottom because he adored the friction against his prostate. When he was a top he needed Viagra to get hard. Sex was a job he did and then forgot by the time he was with his next client, he maintained. The men favored massages, and occasionally put on porno videos. During sex he closed his eyes and thought of women. He knew he helped a lot of men compensate for their loneliness and said he had a gift for making them feel comfortable, even though he would never kiss any of them. His only request from those he frequented was to be respected.

ACTORS AND AGENTS

Shakespeare's actors often doubled as rent boys for extra cash. American actors did it to get roles: David Bret in his book *Clark Gable* and William J. Mann in his book *Wisecracker*, both confirm that **Clark Gable** allowed himself to be anally abused by a 1930s star **William Haines** in exchange for a role. Darwin Porter in his *Paul Newman* writes that **Newman** automatically opened his fly when he saw an easily identifiable glint in a producer's eyes. Donald Spoto wrote in his *The Life of Tennessee Williams, The Kindness of Strangers* that **Warren Beatty** showed up in front of **Williams'** hotel door in a bathrobe: ''You don't have to do that,'' Tennessee reportedly said, although both knew he did. Actor **Jack Buetel** complained that **Howard Hughes** would continually bring him to orgasm in order to drink his virility, which would reinforce, Howard believed, his own, at the same time making sure that Buetel got good roles. Howard Hughes was bisexual, whose father's wealth and his own curiosity led to early sexual discovery. At age 13 he visited Hollywood where a bisexual man and his wife awoke him to every erogenous zone on his body, wrote his biographer Darwin Porter in his excellent *Howard Hughes Hell's Angel*.

Anthony Perkins was an actor who used rent boys on a regular basis and whose supreme happiness was going backstage at strip clubs and visiting the naked lads, commenting later on how they were hung. He could have whomever he wanted, he was told, for a cut-rate $100. This supreme happiness was nonetheless second to his need for anal intercourse, the more animal the better Charles Winecoff writes in his excellent *Antony Perkins--split image*. Winecoff, whose jacket picture shows a writer of great masculine beauty, apparently frequented the same backrooms as Perkins, someone he knew well enough to nod to, on one occasion both of them watching a good-looking exhibitionist whose specialty was pulling out and jacking off his well-proportioned dick.

About **James Dean** several sources said this: ''Jimmy would fuck a snake to get ahead.''

In *Sal Mineo, His Life, Murder and Mystery* its author H. Paul Jeffers writes, ''If he was in the mood for sex with overtones of danger he could find partners in streets where rough hustlers plied their trades.'' At the time **Mineo** was staying at a friend's, his bedroom full of posters of his films and of himself, photographs of naked hunks, a table with gay pornography near the bed, where he would invite good-looking boys for dinner and then an hour or the night in his bedroom (Jeffers mentions one age 14).

It was on the grounds of his carport that he was found stabbed, and a man, described as Italian, was spotted running from the scene. The murder was chalked up as a mystery, and has remained one since.

Mineo's death was immediately linked to the murder of the 1920s and 1930s actor Ramón Novarro, in 1968, by two brothers, hustlers, out to steal what they could, perhaps opposed by Novarro as Mineo had opposed his attacker's attempts at theft. Jeffers states that Sal's friend Peter Falk, *Columbo*, would have cracked the case in two hours.

As this book is about people, I won't go into films that relate aspects of homosexuality, like *My Own Private Idaho, Midnight Cowboy* and *Brokeback Mount*, masterpieces though they are. I do have one regret: In the book *Midnight Express* he hero has sex with his prison mate, while in the *film* Brad Davis shakes his head, a polite No. The denial of the truth of incarceration makes me think of Proust. Had he written the truth about his personages, had he not transformed them into women, he would have written a work of art, and not a never-ending story that few read to the end.

Full Service by Scotty Bowers is a 150-hour interview taped and put in book form by Lionel Frieberg. It's a miracle because Bowers decided to tape his tell-all in 2012 when he was 88. Bowers opened a gas station and because he was a good-looking ex-Marine, always willing to turn an extra buck in the American tradition, he offered himself for rent, and as his clientele increased he hired Marine friends to care for the needs of Hollywood actors, producers, et al., Marines who serviced guys and/or gals, and later women to service guys and other women.

His Marines often had a great time, were served great food around great pools, and did what his clients wanted, which was often just a human presence and a little mutual jerking off. Some of the boys wound up living with the men, as found in the scene from *Some Like It Hot* where Jack Lemmon returns from his date with Osgood and declares to Tony Curtis that he and Osgood were going to get married. ''Why would a guy marry another guy?'' asked Curtis. ''For *security*!'' exclaims Lemmon.

Bowers and his Marines were easy-going guys, and having fun with them must have been fun in itself. I've visited lots of sites on the Net offering male escorts, and the result is extremely disappointing. I've even recovered photos showing some of the Marines employed by Scotty at his gas station. The ones working for Bowers looked like nice, pleasant fellows it would be a pleasure to have a beer with ... and maybe more ... but there isn't one beauty among them. Those found at Net escort agencies are infinitely worse, and whereas Scotty's boys were presentable and sincere looking, those on the Net remind one of vampires without the long canines, some looking drugged and dangerous, but as I haven't seen them all--far from it--there are hopefully exceptions. On the other hand, many of the boys on Net *porn* are gorgeous, veritable *crème de la crème*, or they have something unbelievably enticing about them, while others are so cute and cuddly one would never take them for pros. The best have been found, for years now, at Bel Ami. These boys must cost a fortune that only those in the millionaire class can offer themselves, if, of course, the boys are inclined to sell their bodies.

I'm glad Scotty Bowers existed. I'm glad he lived long enough to tell his tale, as he was 88 in 2012 when the book came out. I'm glad his memory remained so intact and that a publisher dared print a book that includes such men as Tracy, Clift, Perkins, Hughes, Flynn and dozens of others. I wish I could find someone like Scotty and his pals who would ease *my* later years!

Rodolfo Alfonso Raffaello Pierre Filibert Guglielmi di Valentina d'Antonguolla, ''**Valentino**'', was born in 1895. He didn't start off with a life as incredibly adventurous as Errol Flynn's or David Niven's, but he was rough and undisciplined, sent from school to school for being uncontrollable. At first he chose agriculture as his life's work and went to school in Genoa where at 5' 11'' he took up weight-lifting and football. His father had left him money he used to travel to Paris where he went to clubs like the Alcazar and picked up the Apache, a wild dance in which the barely dressed girl was hoisted about, flung like a ragdoll, slapping the male while he threatened her with a knife, she a prostitute, he her pimp. Getting a hard-on with a man showing him the movements, the man loaned Valentino his wife to straighten the boy out, but in the end Valentino got the man.

He found work at Maxim's as a dancer, paid by women per dance. As they were rich, and as he later stated that fucking had always come easily to him, he made good money. He specialized in the tango and had his trousers tailored so as to show his muscular buttocks and extensive manhood. Soon named the Italian Stallion, he thrilled the ladies, who requested private dance lessons. His reputation was augmented when it became known that he was too much of a mouthful for most of them, but just right for a pussy needing stretching.

Valentino

One of Valentino's rich clients was a woman who shot her husband dead, and Rudy, afraid of being dragged into the trial, fled to California. In Los Angeles he hooked up with an actor who convinced him to try out for work as a studio extra.

He became a member of the Torch Club, at around $1,000 a month, that had a special room, # 23, above which was a two-way mirror. New boys were given the room where they fucked in full view of a hidden audience, jacking off. The first boy he went into the room with was Richard Barthelmess, both unaware of the voyeurs. Richard later posed nude for friends and was said to have been huge. Rudy met producers at the club and got numerous small roles. He was soon servicing actresses for money, several a day, and still had enough for Richard whom he continued to see.

Valentino got the chief role in *The Four Horsemen of the Apocalypse* during which Novarro, a bit-player, told him that Valentino was the love of his life. In thanks Valentino gave Novarro a 10" bronze sculpture of his cock, the one Novarro purportedly choked to death on at the end of his kidnapping/murder, whose story follows Valentino's. During a party

Valentino and his girlfriend were introduced as Snow White and Mr. 7 inches, so the exact size of his manhood is unknown.

The success of *The Four Horsemen of the Apocalypse* rocketed him to fame, but he was so imbued with himself that he made increasing demands for more money, causing bad blood among directors and costing him good roles, some of which went to Novarro. He left Metro for Famous Players where his contract went from $350 a week to $750, this during the depression when one earned a dollar a day, if lucky.

The Sheik was an English book found nearly pornographic, about an English woman kidnapped by an Arab who used her for his sexual pleasure in his tent, telling her that she had it better with him than his men, and then the shocking discloser that she ended up liking ''it''. The amusing aspect is that the female lead gave interviews comparing Latin lovers to Americans, although in reality she preferred women and was thought to have been a virgin (to men at least).

His fan mail exploded, with women requesting pubic hair clippings and men underwear he ejaculated in--in return for money. He married. Divorced. And immediately married again, so rapidly that the first marriage hadn't come through and he was indicted for bigamy. He got out of it when his new wife declared their marriage had not been consummated, and was thusly null and void.

His next film was the one he preferred, *Blood and Sand*, he as a matador. He was 26 and apparently loved to wear the matador costume as a preliminary to sex.

In the film *Young Rajah* Valentino played a student who, in one scene where the rowers were wearing shorts and carrying a boat over their heads, was bawled out by the director who thought he was sporting a boner as a prank, and ordered him to take a cold shower. Valentino lowered the shorts to prove that he was in his normal flaccid state.

Valentino was said to have had such magnetism that even homophobes wanted to have sex with him, wrote Jacques Hébertot, whose pleasure was touring French streets to pick up boys that he turned into actors. Hébertot's greatest discovery was Gérard Philipe, one of France's truly great and beloved artists. Hébertot introduced Valentino to André Daven that Hébertot said was the world's most beautiful boy. Stuck on himself, Daven told the great Valentino that if he wanted him he'd have to give him a role in one of his film. Valentino replied that he'd give the boy a role in *all* his films, an anecdote revealed by David Bret in his *Valentino*, a wonderful book, as are all of Bret's works.

Valentino in the middle, Daven on the right
(sorry, it's the best I can do).

In 1923, at age 28, Valentino signed a contract with United Artists that paid $10,000 a week and 42% of Unites Artists' profits, plus a bungalow, a maid, a dresser and a chef. The only provision was that his wife, a harridan, have no say whatsoever concerning the films and the filming of the films. He signed, especially as Daven was still at his side. (After Valentino's death Daven returned to Paris and to Hébertot, and then literally disappeared from the face of the planet.)

Valentino bought a boat, packed with boys, usually nude, and went to Catalina Island. The fun and games continued at his home, Falcon Lair, where Valentino especially liked to fuck on the roof of his car. Valentino declared a "no fuck Friday", Bret tells us, reserved for outings to things like boxing matches. But as soon as midnight struck, it was back home and orgy time.

It was around then that he began suffering from abdominal pains.

He went to Paris where he fell for a ballet choreographer who chose his boy-for-the-night by lining the lads (mostly his dancers) up in a row and measuring their dicks hard. Valentino took part and won for that night. One boy called his endowment Herculean.

His doctors were certain they could successfully operate and cure his abdominal stress. They couldn't. At 31 he was dead. The end of a near-perfect life.

Unknown today, Novarro was an immense star, whose film *Ben Hur* was number one in the box office before being dethroned by *Gone with the Wind!*

In the times of Ramón Novarro and Valentino homosexuality was considered anything from a psychological disorder to a form of sexual perversion, and during Anthony Perkins' years doctors claimed it could be cured. Perkins underwent treatment to change him into a heterosexual, eventually marrying and producing children. To escape being found out Tyron Powers married, as did Valentino two times (in fact, he was prosecuted for bigamy). Novarro always congratulated himself for having escaped the tender trap. To perform with his wife Powers had to take part in orgies where the naked boys, fucking their girls, their hard asses rising and falling, gave Powers the hard-on he needed.

Tired of Valentino's prima donna demands, directors sought a replacement, and Novarro got his chance. He was born in Mexico near enough to the American border to allow him to pick up English, and in 1916, at the age of 17, he went to California to live with family members, passing through customs where he was given a physical examination and deloused. In Los Angeles he tried to find bit-parts in films, while earning money by posing nude in art classes and ushering in theaters. Valentino, around the same age as Novarro, was also at that moment struggling to survive, living off income that came through an escort service where he made money dancing and fucking women.

Ramón got a role in a dancing scene of *The Four Horsemen of the Apocalypse*, in 1921, a film that cost a whopping $608,000 in a time when a film's budget was $60,000, but turned out to be a success only second to Griffith's *The Birth of a Nation* (1915), bringing in $14 million, saving Metro from bankruptcy, and making Valentino a star overnight. Rex Ingram directed the film and sickened by Valentino's ever-increasing demands, said he could replace the mercurial actor with anyone he chose. Valentino left for Famous Players and Ingram signed on Novarro, determined to unseat Valentino. Novarro's career was helped along also thanks to Valentino's continued salary disputes with his new studio (*and* the strong possibility that Novarro was Ingram's lover, eased by the fact that they were only six years apart in age). Ingram starred Novarro in MGM's *The Arab*, which proved a success although Ingram, who hated and was hated by MGM's director Mayer, suffered from depression. Navarro soon had a new house with all the accoutrements of wealth, a swimming pool and sauna.

Goldwyn studios bought the rights to *Ben Hur* for an unheard-of $1 million. Valentino was chosen for the principle role but still embroiled in salary disputes, the role went to Novarro, chosen over John Gilbert, considered a drunk. Homophobe, Mayer apparently knew nothing of Novarro's homosexuality. At a cost of $4 million, the 1925 film would have to rake in $11 million to breakeven, making it the most expensive film until *Gone with the Wind* 14 years later. It eventually earned only $9.4 million.

Novarro and Garbo.

In the looks category, John Gilbert had a stronger virility that made him more acceptable to male audiences, while Valentino's "eye rolling and nostril flaring" as André Soares puts it in his excellent *Beyond Paradise, The Life of Ramón Novarro*, was too androgynous, and Novarro too pretty, for male appreciation. Herbert Howe, Novarro's lover during this time, was a publicist who set out to prove, in print, that his bed partner was a rampant heterosexual.

Howe and Novarro

When Howe and Novarro broke up Howe wrote that Novarro had once said, "I have so little to give," which had exactly been the case, according to Howe.

And then, seven years after his first film, he spoke, as sound came to pictures, and his voice was deemed perfect. He starred in *Mata Hari* with Garbo but little by little male stars like Gable and James Cagney were favored, and due to his declining looks he turned to alcohol, appearing at a party entirely naked. He remained a huge star in Europe and was assailed by fans when he toured Latin America.

Where guys had begged to be in his company, now he went to rent boys, one of whom, identified only as Chuck, procured dozens for the aging Novarro. He would never be involved in a sex scandal, although his drinking led to numerous automobile accidents.

Then he received a phone call from someone who would service him for money. Novarro got a description of the boy's physical attributes and invited him and his brother over to his home. The boys stripped to their briefs and one went into Novarro's bedroom where he beat Novarro, trying to find out where he hid his cash. His brother came in and while he took over the beating, the other brother, in bloodstained shorts, paraded in front of a mirror in one of Novarro's hats, twirling one of his canes. The brothers, 17 and 22, left the house with $20. The autopsy claimed Novarro had died of asphyxiation, the brothers said he had choked on his own blood--but Bowers in his book insists he had been suffocated by a dildo that Valentino had given him years before, an exact replica of Valentino's 10" cock.

One of the brothers committed suicide, the other was jailed, and Ramón Novarro's star was added to Hollywood's Walk of Fame.

At age 36 **William Haines** was arrested for assaulting a 6-year-old child that he had picked up on the beach, had taken home, showered with, and then, on his bed, took the whole of the child's apparatus in his mouth. As a famous president claimed that he committed a sexual act because he could, because he was powerful enough to get away with it, such was the case of the man few of us have ever heard of, a man so well known, so famous, that he was probably the only man on earth who fucked Clark Gable, with Gable's consent when he found out it was the only way to get a role in a film.

Haines was a rarity, too, in daring to flout his difference, and this in the face of L.J. Mayer, head of MGM, a homophobe (or more probably a man who just couldn't understand why a guy wouldn't want a woman--of whom Mayer had many).

When finally forced out of movies, Haines turned to decorating the homes of the rich, at which he was said to have been excellent.

So today Haines is known for Gable, as in the Renaissance the artist, Torrigiano who brought the Renaissance to England, is known to *cognoscenti* mainly as the man who broke Michelangelo's nose.

Haines reigned during the days of silent films, so a list of his film successes will mean nothing today, as even Gloria Swanson's are forgotten, as are those of Valentino (except to men like myself, who can assure you that an amazing number are now on DVD, although some others have been lost).

He ran away from home in Virginia at age 14, already 6' tall, and already with a boyfriend. Both went to Richmond where they found work at a Du Pont plant. Haines made it to N.Y. at age 16 and worked in a rubber factory. He then sold himself, and his friends at the time said he couldn't get enough sex. He returned to Virginia for two years before heading back to the Big Apple.

He took pride in being a rent boy for what society had best in men and women, and was known for being "rascally handsome and devilishly funny," says William J. Mann is his excellent book on Haines, *Wisecracker*.

He got to Hollywood as did many good-looking boys then as today, met and mated Valentino, as did everyone else of beauty. He had Novarro and Cukor, yet his best friend was a woman, Joan Crawford, she who told him that her husband, Douglas Fairbanks Jr., was fucking Lawrence Olivier. Very early on he did something unknown among homosexuals, he found a boy, Jimmy Shields, who brought him contentment, he said, and with whom he would spend the rest of his life (and with whom he would share his rent boys). He became intimate with Gary Cooper who had just had sex with Lawrence Olivier too, and told Haines that he couldn't understand the Englishman who was flaming with desire one moment, a cold fish the next. The only person Haines couldn't stand was Garbo, because although Haines claimed to be a free soul, he nonetheless married to still rumors concerning his homosexuality, whereas Garbo did exactly what she wished, with whomever she wished.

Haines nearly did so too, especially sexually, but when Mayer had to bail him out of jail for turning up drunk with still another sailor or soldier, he told Haines to stop his messing around or he'd tear up his contract. Haines chose the freedom to fuck whomever he wanted.

Cary Grant was as honest as Haines, but decided to play the studio's game by hiding his sexual preferences, thanks to which he went on to become an immense star, one nobody took for being gay.

Then in 1936 came his arrest and trial for child molestation. The author of *Wisecracker* found the boy involved, 60 years later. Yes, the man said, he blew me, but as I told them back then, it didn't do me any harm.

Haines had been found *not* guilty due to incredible circumstances: In court the 6-year-old boy was asked if the man who had touched him was in the room?

Sixty years later the gentleman explained: Haines was sitting across from me. I wanted to tell them all that the man was at the table. So when the prosecutor asked if he was in the court, I said "No", wanting to add, he's *at that table*. But the defense immediately rose and asked to have the case dismissed.

And it was.

Nothing is left of Haines' films. Nothing of his humor. Like Torrigiano who broke Michelangelo's nose, he's known for anally abusing a man who needed a role in a film, and a child whose parents had left him unattended on a beach.

Brad Davis was a physically and sexually abused child, by both parents, who earned a living, when young, as a rent boy in N.Y. called Bobby. He was an alcoholic and took drugs intravenously, starred in Genet's *Querelle* (as a gay sailor in a Fassbinder film) and *Midnight Express*, giving a role of such intensity that I've personally only been able to watch it once, even though it's in my collection of films. He also starred in Joe Orton's play "Entertaining Mr. Sloane", Orton who had his head and face stove in by his boyfriend through jealousy of Orton's successes, who then killed himself. Both men were addicted to rent boys, especially lads in Morocco who would fuck them silly. Brad Davis had a son, Alex, a transsexual born a girl. He kept his last illness a secret so as to continue working to maintain his family, although he was also certainly an extremely private person. He died at age 41.

Brad Davis

A riveting presence, a supernatural beauty and an icon of masculinity, he was the man guys like Hudson and Dean could only dream of becoming.

Brando got a role at age 20 in *I Remember Mama* from playwright John Van Druten who was 43, a man Brando called an old letch, but one who, Brando said, paid him $200 a week to ''suck my noble tool''. Sex for money, in this case under the guise of a role in a play, is rent.

Brando had an alcoholic mother who took on all comers, purportedly even raped by a group of sailors, while his father was a disciplinarian who sent Brando to the Shattuck Military Academy where Marlon was noted for walking bare-ass through the corridors and lying naked on his bed. His first friend had been Wally Cox, a homely kid Brando saved from bullies at age 10 and who was his best friend and some say the only true love of his whole life. They would camp out together and sleep naked under the same tent blanket, giggling into the night. Back then homosexuality was not at all assumed, and what two ten-year-olds could do sexually is dubious. At the Academy Brando had a 14-year-old off-campus companion, Steve Gilmore, he slipped out of the barrack to visit and fuck, a beautiful boy who worshipped Marlon's good looks and superb body, as hard as a rock from summers of digging ditches to make money. Brando was said to have had 28 girls his first year at the Academy, one of whom described his lifting up her skirt, pulling down her panties, and plowing her virgin cunt while she pleaded with him to stop, leaving her bloody when finished. Kicked out of school, he went to N.Y. where he took acting lessons, and where he spent a summer on Fire Island, buck-naked on the beach, following any guy who asked into the bushes where he let himself be serviced. He took a room with Cox whom he obliged to sleep on a dirty mattress outside their bedroom while Brando fucked both sexes. For a time he had a boy he'd remain friends with for years, Carlo Fiore, with whom he picked up a girl who allowed only Brando to fuck her in a barn they found, while Carlo looked on. At one moment Brando reached over to touch Carlo's face, *to see if he was crying!* (You can read Fiore's book, *The Brando I Knew*.)

Brando took on anything, from the ugliest girls with buckteeth to dirty, drugged creeps that needed delousing. The idea was to get his rocks off, the more often the better. The combination of supreme beauty, a wondrous body, total bisexuality, a wanton need to show himself in skin-tight jeans and a t-shirt one size too small--although his preference was bare-ass naked, the reason he preferred any beach anywhere--plus a lust that pushed him to empty his nuts as often as possible--to expulse the sperm that would sour in his balls otherwise, as he himself explained it to friends-- was completely unique in one lad.

Brando in *I Remember Mama*

Added to this was a talent that put him in the category of the very, very great, a talent that spanned films from *A Streetcar Named Desire* to *The Godfather*. As I've barely scratched the surface, the reader can go on to Darwin Porter's *Brando Unzipped*, a colossal 600-page marvel.

Errol Flynn led two lives, both of undaunted courage, like Heracles whose father Zeus had fucked a maiden nonstop for three days in order for the final ejaculation to produce a hero. Errol's dad was a renowned botanist, biologist and zoologist in one of the world botanical wonders, Australia, where Flynn saw first light in mystical Tasmania. His mother was the daughter of a *Bounty* mutineer, through whom Errol inherited his wanderlust. Only the chromosome for fear was lacking, and his hardiness, which amused to his father (usually away teaching at the university), turned his mother irreconcilably against him, whom he referred to as "that cunt" all his life. Like the baby Heracles, at age 3 he was a strong swimmer, at 5 he was playing doctor with girls, and at 6 he stole a rowing boat in hopes of reaching mainland Australia.

At age 15 he went to London with his father to help care for a cargo of duckbilled platypuses. He was enrolled in school there and not only was he extraordinary in swimming and boxing, at age 16 he became Australian Junior Tennis Champion. He was having sex regularly, having started at age 12 with the Flynns' maid. At 17 he struck out for New Guinea because he had read about a gold strike there. Instead he was taken on as the commissioner of sanitation, wearing a white helmet and uniform. At 18 he was placed in charge of a copra plantation but nearly died when he doubled a dose of medicine against the gonorrhea he had contracted, believing it would heal him twice as fast. He went to Papua where he founded a tobacco plantation that failed, and then on to Macao where he made a fortune gambling and where he frequented opium dens. When his money was stolen by his Chinese mistress he returned to Sydney via Ceylon where a rickshaw boy, unhappy because Flynn wouldn't give him a big enough tip, opened him up with his knife, a 9" scar from his balls to his navel that Flynn loved to show one and all by dropping his trousers (like he did, mentioned elsewhere, when he strode through his dressing room, the door open, in full erection, waiting for any boy or girl who would blow him). He returned to Sydney where he bought a sailboat, the *Sirocco*, the name he would give his future boat in California, one he bought when he became an actor and filled with so many girls he didn't even ask their names.

At 6' 2", gorgeous, he had probably had sex with guys before, but it's not certain. What is known is that once established in Hollywood he frequented the Garden of Allah, a place for swimming, dancing, and drinking, with rooms and bungalows for fucking. The proprietress, sensing that he would like boys, offered to set him up. He said he was willing to try anything once, and spent three days holed up with the lad she gave him. From then on the *Sirocco* carried mostly lads that Flynn shared with what he called his best fuck-pal, David Niven, whose early life was nearly as exotic than Flynn's. There were never two males more masculine than Flynn and Niven, and both preferred boys.

The girls on the *Sirocco* were free, while the boys were mostly paid or offered roles in films, and if they were boys Flynn and Niven wanted back, they really did get bit-parts for services rendered. Both Flynn and Niven most probably sold themselves too for roles, but direct proof is lacking. Flynn would specialize in underage girls and boys, and even as a lad in London he would masturbate before a window that gave onto a bus stop used by school girls, which actually got him arrested. As he was to say later, I live for, with and by my balls.

One of Flynn's films was directed by Robert Florey who had been Valentino's lover. One day when Flynn boasted that he could do anything Valentino did, Florey asked him if he could fuck on the roof of his cars too, a predilection of Valentino's that we saw earlier.

As in the Torch Club mentioned above, Flynn too installed a two-way mirror in the ceiling of his home on Mulholland Drive that gave onto a bedroom where boys and girls unknowingly fucked to the pleasure of those looking down, while beating off.

It was around this time that Flynn was tried for sex with an underage girl, but I'll leave off here, while he's still young and full of cum. For readers wishing to know much more, I recommend David Bret's *Errol Flynn, Gentleman Hellraiser*.

I'll go on with the life of **David Niven** without even leaving a double space, so closely were he and Flynn associated in real life. Niven was far more than an actor, which I do *not* mean in a demeaning way concerning actors, it's just that he was truly much more. Niven was a gentleman in the finest sense, and he produced two of the most beautiful sons to ever adorn the earth. He wrote two books, *The Moon is a Balloon* and *Bring on the*

Empty Horses that I've reread several times because they're marvelous. A writer, a humorist, an actor, Niven was truly an excellent human being.

Born in London, he was not accepted to Eton College because of the pranks he was known for in Heatherdown Preparatory School. He went through the Royal Military College at Sandhurst where he entered the Highland Light Infantry. He served for two years in Malta. He was arrested for insubordination when a general asked if there were any questions after having given a discourse on machine guns. Niven asked, "Do you have the time sir, I have an important date I don't wish to miss?" Put in jail, he got his guards drunk on whisky and escaped ... to N.Y. There he sold whisky, had adventures in Cuba, and ended up in Los Angeles. The rest is film history.

Niven ends his last book on a chilling note. He lived in the whereabouts of Antibes in the south of France and one night during a stroll he came across a graveyard of old boats. He was suddenly crushed by the memories of his young, glorious and vibrant years, for in the middle of them all were the remains of a rotting old yacht, the name of which he could just barely make out: *Sirocco*.

Henry Willson was Hollywood's chief agent in the 1950s, agent being a synonym for pimp and/or casting couch. He was called "pure evil" by some, "slime that oozed from under a rock" by another. He searched everywhere for boys to represent: Alan Delon was found dancing in a Cannes disco, Tab Hunter at an ice rink, and **Rock Hudson** sent out pictures of himself to every agent in Hollywood, and only Willson replied. Willson taught his boys how to eat and how to walk, he saw to it that they got lessons in acting, new teeth, tailored clothing, and he got a percentage *and* the sex his boys gave him in exchange. He pimped out the boys and girls in exchange for money and/or favors. He's said to have worshipped Rock Hudson, actually promising him that one day he would be received in the White House, which was the case, while the wealthy Willson ended up in a pauper's grave.

Part of his job was to smother scandals, and he did it so well his boys could participate in pool orgies without fear of discovery, unless it was Willson himself who turned them in. He went so far as to marry his secretary to one of them when the press came close to discovering the actor was gay.

Henry was nonetheless close to actors in more than sex. He befriended them, listened to their stories, gave advice, tons of advice; he protected them and even fathered them. He was known to be honest with his boys: if he slept with one, the lad was assured of getting a role in a film.

Willson himself relates the story of **Rory Calhoun** and **Guy Madison**. Rory was an ex-convict who had began by stealing groceries before working up to jewels and cars. When caught, he was sent to San Quentin, at age 18. Out riding on a horse through the hills above Hollywood after his release, Rory came on a woman who liked his looks and told him she knew an agent that might be interested in representing him. When Henry got to known Rory better he deemed the boy too huge to be accommodated by most men, and anyway Rory had no interest in that kind of sex. Besides, he preferred women when not obliged to sleep with Willson. Guy Madison was also a client of Henry's who had refused intercourse with him because it was not his thing. Then, on a certain rainy day, Willson, lonely, decided to drive out to see Rory. In front of Rory's home Willson recognized the Jaguar belonging to Guy. As he approached the Jag he could see it was wildly rocking. Drawing closer, he saw Calhoun fucking Guy, seemingly impossible because Guy had assured him that he was virgin (in that way) and Henry thought that Rory was simply too big. Later Guy swore that it had been the first time for him, as it had been for Rory (he said, although he had spent years in prison when he was a boy, and we know what *that* means).

Rory Calhoun

Later, when reporters were getting too close to Hudson, who was bringing in a fortune for Willson, some believe Willson turned over documents to the press exposing Rory's imprisonment, in order to get them interested elsewhere. For weeks afterwards Rory was constantly in the news.

Tab Hunter was a kid raised by a single mom. He went to a military academy, was a soda jerk, an usher, and at age 15 he entered the Coast Guard by lying about his age. At 12 he had worked at a riding academy where he met an actor. On furloughs from the Coast Guard he crashed at the actor's apartment. No one knows at what age their affaire began. The actor put the boy on to Willson whose attempts at seduction Hunter *said* he had successfully avoided. But Hunter was later rounded up with 26 other naked guys at a gay pool party, that became known as Tab's Pajama Game when exposed by *Confidential* magazine, which had a circulation of 4 million. Tab was obliged to switch to television. In 2007 he was added to the Hollywood Walk of Fame.

Hunter

As stated elsewhere in this book, blackmail has been a problem throughout the ages, forcing even a wealthy Krupp to commit suicide. Willson's stars were occasionally blackmailed too, and Willson wound up either paying the blackmailers or, preferably, getting them roles in b-films and on t.v. series, making it impossible for them to reveal an actor's homosexuality without revealing their own.

If the reader wishes to learn more about the many stars Willson represented, I suggest *The Man Who Invented Rock Hudson, the Pretty Boys and Dirty Deals of Henry Willson* by Robert Hofler.

George Cukor directed *Gone with the Wind* until replaced, as well as *The Philadelphia Story, Gaslight, Adam's Rib, A Star is Born* and *My Fair Lady*, from 1930 to 1981 when felled by a heart attack. His main source of sex was rent boys, several he put through school, Patrick McGilligan tells us in his *A Double Life--George Cukor*. One boy went on to become a N.Y. literary agent who was eternally grateful to Cukor. Another was made a Beverly Hills accountant after Cukor put him through college. At Christmas all his boys and those working for him received sumptuous gifts, at one Christmas they all got a Picasso pencil drawing.

Cukor's Sunday parties were to die for. As Cukor was afraid to visit gay bars, afraid of being recognized, anyone and everyone of physical beauty was invited on Sunday to his pool, boys picked up literally off the streets, hitchhikers, and boys from gymnasiums. His parties were described as a gay Mecca, the place one had to be to meet the guys they would bed that night and during the coming week. At the parties boys were fed and given a few bucks for immediate service in the garden house or on the grounds.

The life of **Lawrence Olivier** (Larry) is the most startling I've read. He worshipped his brother Dickie with whom he shared the same bed at age 8. He would run home from school in hopes that night would fall so he could bring his Dickie pleasure. Later he told friends that the sex sometimes hurt him but that his aim was to make Dickie happy, yet Larry insisted that a priest was the first to introduce him to anal intercourse, perhaps in an effort to protect Dickie from calumny.

At age 9 he entered a choir where said priest sodomized him, one of thousands who became priests so as to have access to young choirboys, an experience Larry was said to have liked, a reprehensive act that his brother was perhaps aware of but did nothing to stop, especially as he had turned to girls--as reported by Darwin Porter and Roy Moseley in their *Damn You, Scarlet O'Hara, the Private Lives of Vivien Lee and Laurence Olivier*, a 700-page wonder.

He entered St. Edwards School at Oxford at age 14 and admitted later to Noël Coward (who was his lover for many years) that he was the boys' bitch, boys who fucked him repeatedly every night, and as one of them admitted years later: Why not? The teachers were getting their rocks off with *us*! One of the boys, he told Coward, was for him a god who would kiss him tenderly and thank him each time he withdrew from his buttocks.

At 21 Larry became one of many who shared **James Whales** casting couch, the director of *Frankenstein* and *The Invisible Man*. One of Larry's friends said Larry slept with anyone for a role, which places him squarely in the rent-boy category, and Larry himself said that had he done so sooner *he* would have been the star of *Frankenstein* (which would have immensely enriched the film).

Larry sailed to America and Hollywood where he met the gorgeous **Douglas Fairbanks Jr.** and his wife Joan Crawford, who told her friend William Haines, the man Gable allowed to sodomize him for a role, that Larry was, at that very moment, 'being butt-fucked by my husband'', and it was true that at night, for a week, they were inseparable. During this time Crawford had Gable.

Larry and Oberon in A.V. Bramble's 1939 *Wuthering Heights*, clear proof that Olivier was God's gift to man.

In the play *Romeo and Juliette* Larry told John Gielgud that the only way to play Romeo was with a perpetual erection, because all the boy wanted was to get into Juliet's pants. Certainly excellent advice.

Later, much later, it was Sir Lawrence Olivier, well established, who set up his own casting couch as revealed by the budding actor Dan Cunningham who was invited to swim nude with Larry, who examined his family jewels, as Cunningham put it, and Cunningham said he accepted that it would be the only way to make his way in the theater, as so many, many before him.

And life goes on, dear reader, *un Éternel Recommencement.*

POSTSCRIPT

I'm not a rent boy and never have been. Although I've had propositions. Which reminds me of a story, the last in this book of stories, about Abe Lincoln who was certainly never a rent boy either, although he had a friend, a close friend, a good friend, but that's another story in itself.

One day as president he had the visit of a man who handed over an envelope, offered to Lincoln in hopes the man could gain Lincoln's support on some issue vital to him. That day Lincoln's son was present, perhaps too young to understand what the man was up to. He saw his father refuse the envelope, and the man leave.

The next day the man returned, this time with an envelope twice as thick. Again the man exchanged a few words with the boy's father, again he left, carefully inserting the package into his inside jacket pocket. Lincoln watched him leave, a stern expression on his face.

When the man returned the following day it was with an envelope three times as thick as the first day's. He put it coolly on the president's desk, a slight smile playing over his face. This time the seated Lincoln rose, as if in homage. He picked up the envelope calmly, aware of its weight, a heavenliness that must have hurt when Lincoln slapped the man's face with it.

Once the man had gone, the envelope held tightly in his fist, Lincoln's boy eyed his dad quizzically, shrugged his shoulders, and asked Why? Why had he belted the man this time, but not before?

"Because," said Lincoln, still standing, "this time he was too close to my price."

I've never been a rent boy. Sadly, no one even remotely approached my price. I guess I just never made it to the rank of some of the wonders on the market today.

SOURCES

(1) See my book *Greek Homosexuality*.
(2) See my book *TROY*.

The major sources for the Greek and Roman segments of this book are the following:

<u>Herodotus</u> was also contemporary to the events that interest us here. Cicero called him the Father of History, while Plutarch wrote that he was the Father of Lies. His masterpiece is *The Histories*, considered a chef-d'oeuvre, a work that the gods have preserved intact right up to our own day, a divine intervention that would not have surprised a believer like Herodotus (it's also a book I reread every year). Part of his work may have been derived from other sources (what historian's work isn't?) and the facts rearranged in an effort to give them dramatic force and please an audience. Much of what he did was based on oral histories, many of which themselves were based on early folk tales, highly suspect, naturally, in all their details. Aristophanes made fun of segments of his work and Thucydides called Herodotus a storyteller. Surprisingly little is known about his own life. For example, he writes lovingly about Samos, leading some to believe that he may have spent his youth there. Born near Ionia, he wrote in that dialect, learning it perhaps on Samos. He was his own best publicist, taking his works to festivals and games, such as the Olympic Games, and reading them to the spectators. As I've said, many people doubt that he actually went where he said he went and saw what he said he saw. But the same was true of Marco Polo who causes disbelief to this day simply because he never mentioned eating noodles in China or seeing the Great Wall or even drinking Chinese tea. But no historian, then as now, can write a book on ancient occurrences without referring to Herodotus' observations. An amusing example of recent discoveries that give credence to Herodotus is this: Herodotus wrote about a kind of giant ant, the size of a fox, living in India, in the desert, that dug up gold. This was ridiculed until the French ethnologist Peissel came upon a marmot living in today's Pakistan that burrows in the sand and has for generations brought wealth to the region by bringing up gold from its burrows. Peissel suggests that the original confusion came from the fact that the Persian word for marmot was similar to the word for mountain ant.

<u>Lucian</u> (125-180 A.D.) was an Assyrian rhetorician who taught the art of pleading in courts so well that he became both famous and wealthy. He traveled extensively throughout Ionia, Greece, Italy and Gaulle.

<u>Phaedo</u> (4th century B.C.) was a slave of Socrates and perhaps his lover, whom Socrates freed. In Socrates' *Phaedo* Socrates discusses the immortality of the soul, in Phaedo's presence, the night before his suicide for corruption of Athenian youth, in this case for not respecting the gods, Zeus, Hera et al.

Plutarch was born near Delphi around 46 A.D. to a wealthy family. He was married, and a letter to his wife even exists to this day. He had sons, the exact number unknown. He studied mathematics and philosophy in Athens and was known to have visited most of the major Greek sites mentioned in this book, as well as Rome. He personally knew the Emperors Trajan and Hadrian, and became a Roman citizen. He was a high priest at Delphi and his duty consisted of interpreting the auguries of the Pythoness (no mean task). He wrote the *Lives of the Emperors* but alas only two of the lesser emperors survive. Another verily monumental work was *Parallel Lives of Greeks and Romans* of which twenty-three exist. His interest was the destinies of his subjects, how they made their way through the meanders of life. I too have a passionate interest in how men strive their wholes lives for success, only to be crushed, like Alcibiades, like Pericles, at the end. In explanation of his oeuvre Plutarch wrote that what interested him was not history but lives, and the Jekyll/Hyde struggle of virtue versus vice. A small jest, he went on, often reveals more than battles during which thousands die. His writings on Sparta, alongside those of Xenophon, are nearly all we possess concerning that extraordinary city-state. His major biographies are the *Life of Alexander* and the *Life of Julius Caesar*. Amusingly, Plutarch wrote a scathing review of Herodotus' work in which he stated that the great historian was fanatically biased in favor of the Greeks who could do, according to Herodotus, no wrong.

Theophrastus (371-287 B.C.) studied under Plato and took over Aristotle's school the Lyceum for 35 years, until his death at age 85. He was probably the lover of Aristotle's son Nicomachus. He was called the Father of Botany thanks to his interest in plant. His works exist in fragments.

Thucydides was an Athenian general and historian, contemporary with the events he described. What he wrote was based on what actually happened; there was no extrapolating; no divine intervention on the part of the gods as was the case with Plutarch. An example of this was his observation that birds and animals that ate plague victims died as a result, leading him to conclude that the disease had a natural rather than supernatural cause. His description of the plague has never been equaled, the plague that he himself caught while participating in the Peloponnesian War. He is thought to have died in 411 B.C., the date at which his writing suddenly stops. He admired Pericles and democracy but not the radical form found in Athens.

Xenophon, born near Athens in 430 B.C., was a historian and general. His masterpieces are *The Peloponnesian Wars* and *Anabasis*. He loved Sparta and served under Spartan generals during the Persian Wars. Like the Spartans, he believed in oligarchic rule, rule by the few, be they the most intelligent or wealthy or militarily acute. He spent a great deal of time in Persia alongside Cyrus the Younger who raised an army, among whom were Xenophon's 10,000 and other mercenaries (all of which is the subject of *Anabasis*). After Cyrus' death Xenophon and his ten thousand made their way back home, the breathtaking account of which ends his *Anabasis*. The Athenians exiled him when he fought with the Spartans against Athens but the Spartans offered him an estate where he wrote his works. His banishment may have been revoked thanks to his son Gryllus who brilliantly fought and died for Athens.

Of the philosophers, <u>Plato</u> was the major source for this book. Plato's most famous work is the Allegory of the Cave. Humans in the cave have no other reality than the shadows they see on the walls. If they looked around they could see what was casting the shadows and by doing so gain additional knowledge. If they left the cave they would discover the sun, analogous to truth. If those who saw the sun reentered the cave and told the others, they would not be believed. There are thusly different levels of reality that only the wisest are able to see; the others remain ignorant. It's basically thanks to Plato and Xenophon that we know what we do about Socrates. Plato's perfect republic is ruled by the best (an aristocracy), headed by a philosopher king who guides his people thanks to his wisdom and reason. An inferior form of government, one that comes after an aristocracy, is a timocracy, ruled by the honorable. A timocracy is in the hands of a warrior class. Plato has Sparta in mind, but it's unclear how he could have found this form of government better than, for example, a democracy. The problem may be that we know, in reality, so little about Sparta. Next comes an oligarchy based on wealth, followed by a democracy, rule by just anyone and everyone. This degenerates into a tyranny, meaning a government of oppression, because of the conflict between the rich and the poor in a democracy.

As for the tragedians, we'll begin with <u>Sophocles</u>, author of 123 plays of which 7 remain, notably *Oedipus* and *Antigone*. An Athenian born to a rich family just before the Battle of Marathon, he was a firm supporter of Pericles. He fought alongside Pericles against Samos when the island attempted to become autonomous from Athens. He was elected as a magistrate during the Sicilian Expedition led by Alcibiades, and given for function the goal of finding out why the expedition had ended disastrously. Sophocles was always ready and willing to succumb to the charms of boys. Plutarch tells us that even at age 65 ''he led a handsome boy outside the city walls to have his way with him. He spread the boy's poor himation--a rectangular piece of cloth thrown over the left shoulder that drapes the body--upon the ground. To cover them both he spread his rich cloak. After Sophocles took his pleasure the boy took the cloak and left the himation for Sophocles. This misadventure was eventually known to all.'' He died at 90, some say while reciting a very long tirade from *Antigone* because he hadn't paused to take a breath (apocryphal but charming). Another version has him choking on grapes, and a final one has him dying of happiness after winning the equivalent of our Oscar at a festival. The first of his trilogy--called the Theban plays--is *Oedipus the King*. Here the baby Oedipus--in a plot that goes back to Priam and Paris at the founding of Troy--is handed over to a servant to be killed in order to prevent the accomplishment of an oracle, an oracle stating that he will kill his father and marry his mother. He does both after solving the riddle of the sphinx (which creature becomes four-footed, then two-footed and finally three-footed?). His mother, when she finds out she's been bedding her own son, commits suicide and Oedipus blinds himself. In *Oedipus at Colonus* Oedipus dies and we learn more about his children Antigone, Polyneices and Eteocles. In *Antigone* Polyneices is accused of treason and killed. His body is thrown outside the city walls and the king forbids its burial, under pain of death. Antigone does so anyway and, faced with death, she commits suicide, followed by the king's son who was going to wed her, followed by the king's wife who couldn't face losing her precious son. (Whew!)

The father of tragedians was Aeschylus, of whom 7 out of perhaps 90 plays have survived. His gravestone celebrated his heroism during the victory against the Persians at Marathon and *not his plays*, proof of the extraordinary importance of Greek survival against the barbarians (sadly, he lost his brother at Marathon). He is said to have been a deeply religious person, dedicated to Zeus. As a boy he worked in a vineyard until Dionysus visited him in a dream and directed him to write plays. One of his plays supposedly divulged too much about the Eleusinian Mysteries and he was nearly stoned to death by the audience. He had to stand trial but pleaded ignorance. He got off when the judges learned of the death of his brother at Marathon and when Aeschylus showed the wounds he and a second brother had received at Marathon too, the second brother left with but a stump in place of his hand. In one of his later plays, Pericles was part of the chorus. The subjects of his plays often concerned Troy and the Persian Wars, Marathon, Salamis and Xerxes (Xerxes is accused of losing the war due to hubris; his building of the bridge over the Hellespont was a show of arrogance the gods found unacceptable). In *Seven against Thebes* he too tells about Oedipus' two sons. This time the boys agree to become kings of Thebes on alternate years. Naturally, when the time comes for them to change places the king in place refuses, which leads to both boys killing each other. *Agamemnon* is an excellent retelling of the Trojan War, as Agamemnon sails home to be murdered by his wife Clytemnestra. In *The Libation Bearers* Agamemnon's boy Orestes returns home to destroy his father's assassins, Clytemnestra and her lover Aegisthus. In *The Eumenides* (the Kindly Spirits) Orestes is chased by the Furies for having killed his mother. He takes shelter with Apollo who decides, with Athena, to try the boy before a court. The vote is a tie, but Athena, preaching the importance of reason and understanding, acquits him. She then changes the terrible Furies into sweet Eumenides.

Euripides may have written 90 plays of which 18 survive. His approach was a study of the inner lives of his personages, the predecessor, therefore, of Shakespeare. Due to his stance on certain subjects, he thought it best to leave Athens voluntarily rather than suffer an end similar to that of Socrates. An example: ''I would prefer to stand three times to confront my enemies in battle rather than bear a single child!'' He was born on the island of Salamis, of Persian-War fame; in fact he was born on the very day of the battle. His youth was spent in athletics and dance. Due to bad marriages with unfaithful wives, he withdrew to Salamis where he wrote while contemplating sea and sky. When Sparta defeated Athens in war, it did not destroy the city-state. Plutarch states that this was thanks to one of Euripides' plays, *Electra*, put on for the Spartans in Athens, a play they found so wonderful that they proclaimed that it would be barbarous to destroy a city capable of engendering men of the quality of Euripides. (The real reason was to preserve the city that had twice saved Greece from Persian victory.) Euripides was known for his love of Agathon, a youth praised for his beauty as well as for his culture, and would later become a playwright. Aristophanes mocked Euripides for loving Agathon long after he had left his boyhood behind him. (Remember, not everyone followed boy-love to the letter. The idea of men loving boys until they grew whiskers did not always hold true. Boys grown ''old'' could shave their chins and butts; some men just preferred other men, hairy or not; most men impregnated boys but other men adored being penetrated.) Plato says that Agathon had polished manners, wealth, wisdom and dispensed hospitality with ease and refinement.

Aristophanes, my preferred playwright, is, naturally, the father of comedy. He wrote perhaps 40 plays of which 11 remain. He was feared by all: Plato states that it was his play *The Clouds* the root of the trial that cost Socrates his life. Nearly nothing is known about him other than what he himself revealed in his works. Playwrights were obliged to be conservative because part of each play was funded by a wealthy citizen, an honor for the citizen and a caveat for the author. He was an exponent of make-love-not-war who saw his country go from its wonderful defeat of the Persians to its end at the hands of the Spartans. Along with Alcibiades and Socrates, Aristophanes is featured in Plato's *The Symposium* in which he is gently mocked, proof that he was considered, even by those he poked fun at, as affable. *The Acharnians* highlights the troubles the Athenians went through after the death of Pericles and their defeat at the hands of Sparta. *The Peace* focuses on the Peace of Nicias. *Lysistrata* tells about the plight of women trying to bring about peace in order to prevent the sacrifice of their sons during war, occasioning the world's first sex strike. When Athens lost its freedom to Sparta, Aristophanes stopped writing plays.

Other key sources are: <u>Athenaeus</u> who lived in the times of Marcus Aurelius (meaning we know little about him). His *Deipnosopistae* is a banquet conversation *à la Platon* during which conversations on every possible subject took place, filling fifteen books that have come down to us. <u>Isocrate</u> was a student of Socrates who wrote a speech in the defense of Alcibiades during a trial that took place after his death. <u>Cornelius Nepos</u> was a Roman friend of Cicero. Most of what he wrote was lost, so what we know comes through passages of his works in the books of other historians. <u>Andocides</u> was implicated in the Hermes scandal and saved his skin by turning against Alcibiades in a speech that has come down to us called, what else?, *Against Alcibiades*. <u>Lysias</u> was extremely wealthy and contemporary with Alcibiades. He founded a new profession, logographer, which consisted of writing speeches delivered in law courts. One of his speeches was *Against Andocides*, another was *Against Alcibiades*. <u>Diodorus Siculus</u> who lived around 50 B.C. and wrote *Historical Library*, consisting of forty volumes. <u>Pausanias</u>, a Greek historian and geographer, famous for his *Description of Greece*. He was contemporary with Hadrian and Marcus Aurelius. He's noted as being someone interested in everything, careful in his writing and scrupulously honest. <u>Simonides of Ceos</u> was a Greek poet born about 550 B.C. Besides his poems, he added four letters to the Greek alphabet. <u>Bion</u> was a Greek philosopher known for his diatribes, satires and attacks on religion. He lived around 300 B.C. <u>Ovid</u> lived around 10 B.C. A Roman poet especially known for his *Metamorphoses*, one of the world's most important sources of classical mythology. <u>Polybius</u> was a Greek historian born in Arcadia around 200 B.C. His work describes the rise of the Roman Republic and he is known for his ideas on the separation of powers in government. <u>Aelianus</u> was a Roman author and teacher of rhetoric who spoke and wrote in Greek. <u>Philemon</u> lived to be a hundred but alas only fragments of his works remain. He must have been very popular as he won numerous victories as a poet and playwright. The Greek poet <u>Anacreon</u> was born in 582 B.C. and was known for his drinking songs. <u>Eupolis</u> lived around 430 B.C. An Athenian poet who lived and wrote during the Peloponnesian Wars. <u>Phanocles</u> lived during the time of Alexander the Great. He was the author of a poem on boy-love that described the love of Orpheus for Calais, and his death at the hands of Thracian women. <u>Mimnermus</u> was born in Ionian Smyrna around 630 B.C. He wrote short love poems suitable for performance at drinking parties. <u>Polyenus</u> was a Macedonian known as a rhetorician and for his books on war strategies. <u>Cicero</u> was born in 106 B.C. and murdered by Mark Antony in 43 B.C. Michael Grant said it all when he wrote, ''the influence of Cicero upon the history of European literature and ideas greatly exceeds that of any other prose writer in any language."

A special mention for Pindar, Theognis and Theocritus. <u>Pindar</u>'s great love was Theoxenus of Tenodos about whom he wrote: "Whosoever, once he has seen the rays flashing from the eyes of Theoxenus, and is not shattered by the waves of desire, has a black heart forged of a cold flame. Like wax of the sacred bees, I melt when I look at the young limbs of boys." He lived around 500 B.C. and celebrated the Greek victories against the Persians at Salamis and Plataea. His home in Thebes became a must for his devotees.

<u>Theognis</u> was born around 550 B.C. His poems consist of maxims and advice as to how to live life. Fortunately, a great deal of his work has come down to us, most of which is dedicated to his beloved, the handsome Cyrnus.

<u>Theocritus</u> was a Sicilian and lived around 270 B.C. I've given a short extract from one of Theocritus' works in the chapter on Socrates, a poem thought so vile that it was put in Latin in Renaissance books. In his 7th Idyll Aratus is passionately in love with a lad. His 12th Idyll refers to Diocles who died saving the life of Philolaus, the boy he loved, and in whose honor kissing contests were held every spring at his tomb. In his 23rd Idyll a lover commits suicide because of unrequited love, warning his belovèd that one day he too will burn and weep for a cruel boy. Before hanging himself the lover kissed the doorpost from which he would attach the noose. The boy treated the corpse with disdain and went off to the gymnasium for a swim where a statue of Eros fell on him, coloring the water with his blood. In his 29th Idyll a lover warns his belovèd that he too will age and his beauty will lose its freshness. He is therefore advised to show more kindness as "you will one day be desperate for a beautiful young man's attentions." Although lads are often disappointing, it is impossible not to fall madly in love with them. In the 30th Idyll the poet states that when a man grows old he should keep a distance from boys, but in his heart he knows that the only alternative to loving a boy is simply to cease to exist.

OTHER SOURCES

Abbott Jacob, *History of Pyrrhus*, 2009.
Ady, Cecilia, *A History of Milan under the Sforza,* 1907.
Aldrich and Wotherspoon, *Who's Who in Gay and Lesbian History,* 2001.
Aristophanes, Bantam Drama, 1962.
Aronson, Marc, *Sir Walter Ralegh*, 2000.
Baglione, *Caravaggio,* circa 1600.
Baker Simon, *Ancient Rome*, 2006.
Barber, Richard, *The Devil's Crown--Henry II and Sons*, 1978.

Barber, Stanley, *Alexandros*, 2010.
Beachy, Robert, *Gay Berlin*, 2014. Marvelous.
Bellori, *Caravaggio*, circa 1600.
Bergreen, Laurence, *Over the Edge of the World. Magellan.* 2003.
Bret, David, *Valentino*, 1998.
Bret, David, *Errol Flynn, Gentleman Hellraiser*, 2004
Bret, David, *Clark Gable*, 2007.
Bret, Davis, *Trailblazers*, 2009.
Bicheno, Hugh, *Vendetta*, 2007.
Bierman, John, *Dark Safari, Henry Morton Stanley*, 1990.
Boyd, Douglas, *April Queen*, 2004.
Boyles, David, *Blondel's Song*, 2005.
Bramly, Serge, *Leonardo*, 1988. A wonderful book.
Bury and Meiggs, *A History of Greece*, 1975.
Calimach, Andrew, *Lover's Legends*, 2002.
Callow, Simon, *Charles Laughton*, 1995.
Carroll, Stuart, *Maryrs & Murderers, The Guise Family*, 2009.
Cawthorne, Nigel, *Sex Lives of the Popes*, 1996.
Cellini, Benvenuto, *The Autobiography of Benvenuto Cellini.*
Ceram, C.W., *Gods, Graves and Scholars*, 1951.
Chamberlin, E.R. *The Fall of the House of Borgia*, 1974.
Cloulas, Ivan, *The Borgia*, 1989.
Cooper, John, *The Queen's Agent*, 2011.
Crompton, Louis, *Byron and Greek Love*, 1985.
Crouch, David, *William Marshal*, 1990.
Crowley, Roger, *Empires of the Sea*, 2008. Marvelous.
Curtis Cate, *Friedrich Nietzsche*, 2002.
Dale, Richard, *Who Killed Sir Walter Ralegh?*, 2011.
Dalrymple, William, *The Last Mughal*, 2006.
Davidson, James, *Courtesans and Fishcakes*, 1998.
Davidson, James, *The Greeks and Greek Love*, 2007.
Davis, John Paul, *The Gothic King, Henry III*, 2013.
Defored, Frank, *Big Bill Tilden*, 1975.
Dover K.J. *Greek Homosexuality*, 1978.
Duby, George, *William Marshal*, 1985.
Eisler, Benita, *BYRON Child of Passion, Fool of Fame*, 2000. Wonderful.
Evans, Robert, *The Kid Stays in the Picture*, 1994.
Everitt Anthony, *Augustus*, 2006.
Everitt Anthony, *Cicero*, 2001.
Everitt, Anthony, *Hadrian*, 2009.
Fagles, Robert, *The Iliad*, 1990.
Fiore, Carlo, *The Brando I Knew*, 1974.
Forellino, Antonio, *Michelangelo*, 2005. Beautiful reproductions.

Fothergill, Brian, *Beckford of Fonthill*, 1979.
Frieda, Leonie, *Catherine de Medici*, 2003. Wonderful.
Gayford, Martin, *Michelangelo*, 2013. A beautiful book.
Gillingham, John, *Richard the Lionheart*, 1978.
Gilmore, John, *Live Fast—Die Young*, 1997.
Gilmore, John, *Laid Bare*, 1997.
Goldsworthy Adrian, *Caesar*, 2006
Goldsworthy Adrian, *The Fall of Carthage*, 2000.
Goodman Rob and Soni Jimmy, *Rome's Last Citizen*, 2012.
Graham-Dixon, Andrew, *Caravaggio* 2010. Fabulous.
Grant Michael, *History of Rome*, 1978.
Graves, Robert, *Greek Myths*, 1955.
Grazia, Sebastian de, *Machiavelli in Hell*, 1989.
Guicciardini, *Storie fiorentine (History of Florence)*, 1509. Essential.
Halperin David M. *One Hundred Years of Homosexuality*, 1990.
Harris Robert, *Imperium*, 2006.
Herodotus, *The Histories*, Penguin Classics.
Hesiod and Theognis, Penguin Classics, 1973.
Hibbert, Christopher, *Florence, the Biography of a City*, 1993.
Hibbert, Christopher, *The Borgias and Their Enemies*, 2009.
Hibbert, Christopher, *The Great Mutiny India 1857*, 1978. Fabulous.
Hibbert, Christopher, *The Rise and Fall of the House of Medici*, 1974.
Hicks, Michael, *Richard III*, 2000.
Hine, Daryl, *Puerilities*, 2001.
Hochschild, Adam, *King Leopold's Ghost*, 1999.
Hofler, Robert, *The Man Who Invented Rock Hudson*, 2005.
Hofler, Robert, *Party Animals*, 2010.
Holland Tom, *Rubicon*, 2003.
Hughes Robert, *Rome*, 2011.
Hughes-Hallett, *Heroes*, 2004.
Hughes, Robert, *The Fatal Shore*, 1987.
Hulot, Frédéric, *Suffren, l'Amiral Satan*, 1994.
Hutchinson, Robert, *Elizabeth's Spy Master*, 2006.
Hutchinson, Robert, *House of Treason*, 2009.
Hutchinson, Robert, *Thomas Cromwell*, 2007.
Jack Belinda, *Beatrice's Spell*, 2004.
Jeal, Tim, *Explorers of the Nile*, 2011. Wonderful.
Jeal, Tim, *STANLEY*, 2007. All of Jeal's books are must-reads.
Jeffers, H. Paul, Sal Mineo, *His Life, Murder and Mystery*, 2000.
Johnson, Marion, *The Borgias*, 1981.
Kanfer, Stefan, *Marlon Brando*, 2008.
Köhler, Joachim, *Zarathustra's Secret*, 1989.
Korda, Michael, *HERO The Life and Legend of Lawrence of Arabia*, 2010.

Lacey, Robert, *Henry VIII*, 1972.
Lacy, Robert, *Sir Walter Ralegh*, 1973.
Lambert, Gilles *Caravaggio*, 2007.
Landucci, Luca, *A Florentine Diary*, around 1500, a vital source.
Lev, Elizabeth, *The Tigress of Forli*, 2011. Wonderfully written.
Levy, Buddy, *Conquistador*, 2009.
Levy, Buddy, *River of Darkness*, 2011. Fabulous.
Lévy, *Edmond, Sparte, 1979.*
Lewis, Bernard, *The Assassins*, 1967.
Livy, *Rome and the Mediterranean*
Livy, *The War with Hannibal.*
Lubkin, Gregory, *A Renaissance Court*, 1994.
Lyons, Mathew, *The Favourite*, 2011.
Macintyre, Ben, *The Man Who Would Be King*, 2004.
Mackay, James, *In My End is My Beginning, Mary Queen of Scots*, 1999.
Mallett, Michael and Christine Shaw, *The Italian Wars 1494-1559.*
Malye, Jean, *La Véritable Histoire d'Alcibiade*, 2009.
Manchester, William, *A World Lit Only By Fire*, 1993.
Mancini, *Caravaggio*, circa 1600.
Mann, William, *Wisecracker*, 1998.
Marchand, Leslie, *Byron*, 1971.
Martines, Lauro, *April Blood-Florence and the Plot against the Medici*, 2003.
Matyszak, Philip, *The Mithridates the Great*, 2008.
McBrien, William, *Cole Porter*, 2000.
McCann, Graham, *Rebel Males*, 1991.
McGilligan, Patrick, *A Double Life--George Cukor*, 1991.
McLynn, Frank, *Richard and John, Kings of War*, 2007. Fabulous.
McLynn, *Marcus Aurelius*, 2009.
McLynn, *STANLEY, The making of an African explorer*, 1989.
Meier, Christian, *Caesar*, 1996.
Meyer, G.J. *The Borgias, The Hidden History*, 2013.
Meyer, G.J. *The Tudors*, 2010.
Meyer, Jack, *Alcibiades*, 2009.
Miles Richard, *Ancient Worlds*, 2010.
Miles Richard, *Carthage Must be Destroyed*, 2010.
Miller, David, *Richard the Lionheart*, 2003.
Minichiello, Victor and John Scott, *Male Sex Work and Society*, 2014.
Moore Lucy, *Amphibious Thing*, 2000.
Mortimer, Ian, 1415, *Henry V's Year of Glory*, 2009.
Nicholl, Charles, *The Reckoning*, 2002.
Noel, Gerard, *The Renaissance Popes*, 2006.
Opper Thorsten, *Hadrian*, 2008.
Opper, Thorsten, *Hadrian, Empire and Conflict*, 2008.

Parish, James Robert, *The Hollywood Book of Death*, 2002.
Parker, Derek, *Cellini*, 2003, the book is beautifully written.
Payne, Robert and Nihita Romanoff, *Ivan the Terrible*, 2002.
Pernot, Michel, *Henri III*, Le Roi Décrié, 2013, Excellent book.
Peyrefitte, Roger, *Alexandre*, 1979.
Plutarch's Lives, Modern Library.
Pollard, .J., *Warwick the Kingmaker*, 2007.
Polybius, *The Histories*.
Porter, Darwin, *Brando Unzipped*, 2004.
Porter, Darwin, *Paul Newman*, 2009. (All Porter books are fabulous.)
Porter, Darwin, *Howard Hughes*, 2010.
Porter, Darwin & Roy Moseley, *Damn You, Scarlett O'Hara*, 2011.
Read, Piers Paul, *The Templars*, 1999.
Reed, Jeremy, *The Dilly*, 2014.
Reid, B.L., *The Lives of Roger Casement*, 1976.
Renucci Pierre, *Caligula*, 2000.
Reston, James, *Warriors of God, Richard and the Crusades*, 2001.
Rice, Edward, *Captain Sir Richard Francis Burton*, 1990.
Ridley, Jasper, *The Tudor Age*, 1998.
Robb, Peter, M – *The Man Who Became Caravaggio*, 1998.
Robb, Peter, *Street Fight in Naples*, 2010.
Rocco, Antonio, *Alcibiade Enfant à l'Ecole*, 1630.
Rocke, Michael, *Forbidden Friendships*, 1996. Fabulous/indispensible.
Romans Grecs et Latin, Gallimard, 1958.
Ross, Charles, *Richard III*, 1981.
Rouse, W.H.D., Homer's *The Iliad*, 1938.
Royle, Trevor, *Fighting Mac, The Downfall of Sir Hector Macdonald*.
Ruggiero, Guido, *The Boundaries of Eros*, 1985.
Russo, William/Jan Merlin, *MGM Makes Boys Town*, 2012.
Sabatini, Rafael, *The Life of Cesare Borgia*, 1920.
Saslow, James, *Ganymede in the Renaissance*, 1986.
Schiff, Stacy, *Cleopatra*, 2010.
Setz, Wolfram, *The Sins of the Cities of the Plain*, 1881.
Seward, Desmond, *Caravaggio – A Passionate Life*, 1998.
Simonetta, Marcello, *The Montefeltro Conspiracy*, 2008. Wonderful.
Skidmore, Chris, *Death and the Virgin*, 2010.
Skidmore, *Death and the Virgin*, 2007.
Soares, André, *The Life of Ramon Novarro*, 2010.
Solnon, Jean-Fançois, *Henry III*, 1996.
Spoto, Donald, *The Life of Tennessee Williams, The Kindness of Strangers*, 1985.
Stirling, Stuart, *Pizarro Conqueror of the Inca*, 2005.
Strathern, Paul, *The Medici, Godfathers of the Renaissance*, 2003. Superb.

Strauss Barry, *The Spartacus War*, 2009.
Stuart, Stirling, *Pizarro - Conqueror of the Inca*, 2005.
Suetonius, *The Twelve Caesar.s*
Tacitus, *The Annals of Imperial Rome.*
Tacitus, *The Histories.*
Terry, Paul, *In Search of Captain Moonlite*, 2013.
Thucydides, *The Peloponnesian War,* Penguin Classics.
Tibullus, *The Elegies of Tibullus*, translated by Theodore C. Williams
Turner, Ralph, *Eleanor of Aquitaine*, 2009.
Unger Miles, *Magnifico, The Brilliant Life and Violent Time.s*
Unger, Miles, *Machiavelli*, 2008.
Vasari, We would know next to nothing if it were not for him.
Vernant, Jean-Pierre, *Mortals and Immortals*, 1991.
Virgil, *The Aeneid*, Everyman's Library, Knopf, 1907.
Viroli, Maurizio, *Niccolo's Smile, A Biography of Machiavelli*, 1998.
Ward-Perkins Bryan, *The Fall of Rome*, 2005
Warren, W.L., *Henry II*, 1973.
Weir, Alison, *Eleanor of Aquitaine*, 1999. Weir is a fabulous writer.
Weir, Alison, *Mary, Queen of Scots*, 2003.
Weir, Alison, *The Wars of the Roses*, 1995.
Wheaton James, *Spartacus*, 2011.
Wikipedia: Research today is impossible without the aid of this monument.
Williams Craig A. *Roman Homosexuality*, 2010.
Williams John, *Augustus*, 1972.
Wilson, Derek, *The Uncrowned Kings of England*, 2005.
Winecoff, Charles, *Anthony Perkins, split image*, 1996.
Wright, Ed, *History's Greatest Scandals*, 2006.
Wroe, Ann, *Perkin, A Story of Deception*, 2003. Fabulous
Xenophon, *A History of My Times*, Penguin Classics.
Xenophon, *The Persian Expedition*, 1949.

All pictures are from Wikipedia.
Jacket picture of Greek plate from Wikipedia.

Printed in Great Britain
by Amazon